Grades 3–4

THE SUPER SOURCE®

Base Ten Blocks

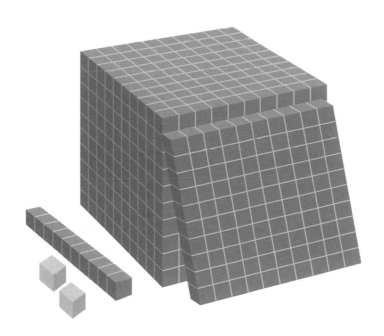

ETA/Cuisenaire®
Vernon Hills, IL

ETA/Cuisenaire® extends its warmest thanks to the many teachers and students across the country who helped ensure the success of The SUPER SOURCE® series by participating in the outlining, writing, and field testing of the materials.

Executive Editor: Doris Hirschhorn
Editorial Manager: John Nelson
Project Writers: Sandy Oringel, Robin Usyk
Project Editor: Harriet Slonim
Field Test Coordinator: Laurie Verdeschi

Design Director: Phyllis Aycock
Production/Manufacturing Coordinator: Roxanne Knoll
Cover Design: Stacy Tisci, David Jensen
Illustrations: Rebecca Thornburgh

The SUPER SOURCE® Base Ten Blocks Grades 3–4
ETA 75372
ISBN 978-1-57452-178-8

ETA/Cuisenaire • Vernon Hills, IL 60061-1862
800-445-5985 • www.etacuisenaire.com

Printed in the United States of America.

07 08 09 10 11 12 13 14 15 16   10 9 8 7 6 5 4 3 2 1

Table of Contents

The Super Source is a series of books, each of which contains a collection of activities to use with a specific math manipulative. Driving **the Super Source** is ETA/Cuisenaire's conviction that children construct their own understandings through rich, hands-on mathematical experiences. Although the activities in each book are written for a specific grade range, they all connect to the core of mathematics learning that is important to every K–6 child. Thus, the material in many activities can easily be refocused for children at other grade levels. Because the activities are not arranged sequentially, children can work on any activity at any time.

The lessons in **the Super Source** all follow a basic structure consistent with the vision of mathematics teaching described in the *Curriculum and Evaluation Standards for School Mathematics* published by the National Council of Teachers of Mathematics. All of the activities in this series involve Problem Solving, Communication, Reasoning, and Mathematical Connections—the first four NCTM Standards. Each activity also focuses on one or more of the following curriculum strands: Number, Geometry, Measurement, Patterns/Functions, Probability/Statistics, and Logic.

HOW LESSONS ARE ORGANIZED

At the beginning of each lesson you will find, to the right of the title, both the major curriculum strands to which the lesson relates and the particular topics that children will work with. Each lesson has three main sections. The first, GETTING READY, offers an *Overview,* which states what children will be doing and why, and provides a list of "What You'll Need." Specific numbers of Base Ten Blocks are suggested on this list but can be adjusted as the needs of your specific situation dictate. Before an activity, blocks can be counted out and placed in containers or self-sealing plastic bags for easy distribution. When crayons are called for, it is understood that markers may be used instead. Blackline masters that are provided for your convenience at the back of the book are also referenced on this materials list. Paper, pencils, scissors, tape, and materials for making charts, which may be necessary in certain activities, are usually not.

Although overhead Base Ten Blocks and the suggestion to make overhead transparencies of the blackline masters are always listed in "What You'll Need" as optional, these materials are highly effective when you want to demonstrate the use of Base Ten Blocks. As you move blocks on the screen, children can work with the same materials at their seats. If overhead Base Ten Blocks are not available, you may want to make and use transparencies of the Base Ten Block shapes and a place-value mat. Children can also use the overhead Base Ten Blocks and/or a transparency of the place-value mat to present their work to other members of their group or to the class.

The second section, THE ACTIVITY, first presents a possible scenario for *Introducing* the children to the activity. The aim of this brief introduction is to help you give children the tools they will need to investigate independently. However, care has been taken to avoid undercutting the activity itself. Since these investigations are designed to enable children to increase their own mathematical power, the idea is to set the stage but not steal the show! The heart of the lesson, *On Their Own,* is found in a box at the top of the second page of each lesson. Here, rich problems stimulate many different problem-solving approaches and lead to a variety of solutions. These hands-on explorations have the potential for bringing children to new mathematical ideas and deepening skills.

On Their Own is intended as a stand-alone activity for children to explore with a partner or in a small group. Be sure to make the needed directions clearly visible. You may want to write them on the chalkboard or on an overhead or present them either on reusable cards or paper. For children who may have difficulty reading the directions, you can read them aloud or make sure that at least one "reader" is in each group.

The last part of this second section, *The Bigger Picture,* gives suggestions for how children can share their work and their thinking and make mathematical connections. Class charts and children's recorded work provide a springboard for discussion. Under "Thinking and Sharing" there are several prompts that you can use to promote discussion. Children will not be able to respond to these prompts with one-word answers. Instead, the prompts encourage children to describe what they notice, tell how they found their results, and give the reasoning behind their answers. Thus children learn to verify their own results rather than relying on the teacher to determine if an answer is "right" or "wrong." Though the class discussion might immediately follow the investigation, it is important not to cut the activity short by having a class discussion too soon.

The Bigger Picture often includes a suggestion for a "Writing" (or drawing) assignment. This is meant to help children process what they have just been doing. You might want to use these ideas as a focus for daily or weekly entries in a math journal that each child keeps.

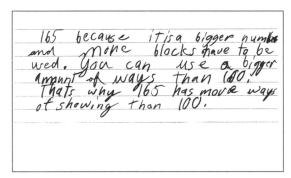

From: *How Many Ways?*

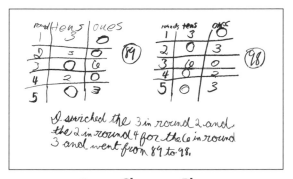

From: *Choose a Place*

The Bigger Picture always ends with ideas for "Extending the Activity." Extensions take the essence of the main activity and either alter or extend its parameters. These activities are well used with a class that becomes deeply involved in the primary activity or for children who finish before the others. In any case, it is probably a good idea to expose the entire class to the possibility of, and the results from, such extensions.

The third and final section of the lesson is TEACHER TALK. Here, in *Where's the Mathematics?,* you can gain insight into the underlying mathematics of the activity and discover some of the strategies children are apt to use as they work. Solutions are also given—when such are necessary and/or helpful. Because *Where's the Mathematics?* provides a view of what may happen in the lesson as well as the underlying mathematical potential that may grow out of it, this may be the section that you want to read before presenting the activity to children.

USING THE ACTIVITIES

The Super Source has been designed to fit into the variety of classroom environments in which it will be used. These range from a completely manipulative-based classroom to one in which manipulatives are just beginning to play a part. You may choose to use some activities in *the Super Source* in the way set forth in each lesson (introducing an activity to the whole class, then breaking up the class into groups that all work on the same task, and so forth). You will then be able to circulate among the groups as they work to observe and perhaps comment on each child's work. This approach requires a full classroom set of materials but allows you to concentrate on the variety of ways that children respond to a given activity.

Alternatively, you may wish to make two or three related activities available to different groups of children at the same time. You may even wish to use different manipulatives to explore the same mathematical concept. (Snap™ Cubes and Cuisenaire® Rods, for example, can be used to teach some of the same principles as Base Ten Blocks.) This approach does not require full classroom sets of a particular manipulative. It also permits greater adaptation of materials to individual children's needs and/or preferences.

If children are comfortable working independently, you might want to set up a "menu"—that is, set out a number of related activities from which children can choose. Children should be encouraged to write about their experiences with these independent activities.

However you choose to use *the Super Source* activities, it would be wise to allow time for several groups or the entire class to share their experiences. The dynamics of this type of inter-action, where children share not only solutions and strategies but also feelings and intuitions, is the basis of continued mathematical growth. It allows children who are beginning to form a mathematical structure to clarify it and those who have mastered just isolated concepts to begin to see how these concepts might fit together.

Again, both the individual teaching style and combined learning styles of the children should dictate the specific method of utilizing *the Super Source* lessons. At first sight, some activities may appear too difficult for some of your children, and you may find yourself tempted to actually "teach" by modeling exactly how an activity can lead to a particular learning outcome. If you do this, you rob children of the chance to try the activity in whatever way they can. As long as children have a way to begin an investigation, give them time and opportunity to see it through. Instead of making assumptions about what children will or won't do, watch and listen. The excitement and challenge of the activity—as well as the chance to work cooperatively—may bring out abilities in children that will surprise you.

If you are convinced, however, that an activity does not suit your students, adjust it, by all means. You may want to change the language, either by simplifying it or by referring to specific vocabulary that you and your children already use and are comfortable with. On the other hand, if you suspect that an activity isn't challenging enough, you may want to read through the activity extensions for a variation that you can give children instead.

RECORDING

Although the direct process of working with Base Ten Blocks is a valuable one, it is afterward, when children look at, compare, share, and think about their constructions and arrangements, that an activity yields its greatest rewards. However, because Base Ten Block activity results can't always be left intact for very long, children need an effective way to record their work. To this end, at the back of this book recording paper is provided for reproduction. The "What You'll Need" listing at the beginning of each lesson often specifies the kind of recording paper to use. For example, in an activity where children are working only with units, longs, and flats, they can duplicate their work or trace the block pieces on the Base Ten Block Grid Paper (1-centimeter grid paper) found on page 96.

From: *Riddle Me This*

From: *In a Row*

From: *It's in the Bag*

You may want to have some children record their work on 2-centimeter grid paper to provide them with larger areas to color. Other children may be able to use grids with squares that are even smaller than 1 square centimeter. These children may also be able to use the blocks as templates to trace their results on unlined paper.

When young children initially explore with Base Ten Blocks, they are likely to use up every available block in making a huge pattern. A pattern of this size can be daunting for a child to record. Such patterns may be recorded using cutouts of the Base Ten Block shapes. (You may wish to fill a sheet of Base Ten Block Grid Paper with outlines of flats, longs, and units. Then you can reproduce the sheet and cut the shapes apart.) Children can color the shapes and paste them in place on unlined paper.

Another interesting way to "freeze" a Base Ten Block design or construction is to create it using the appropriate software and then print it. Children can use a classroom or resource-room computer if it is available or, where possible, extend the activity into a home assignment by utilizing their home computers.

Recording involves more than copying the designs. Writing, drawing, and making charts and tables are also ways to record. By creating a table of data gathered in the course of their investigations, children are able to draw conclusions and look for patterns. When children write or draw, either in their group or later by themselves, they are clarifying their understanding of their recent mathematical experience.

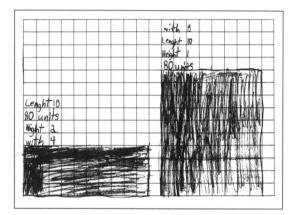

From: *Building Boxes*

From: *School Sizes*

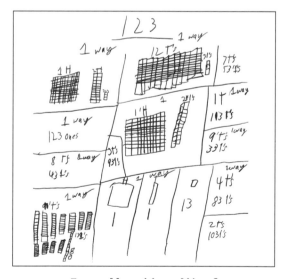

From: *How Many Ways?*

With a roomful of children busily engaged in their investigations, it is not easy for a teacher to keep track of how individual children are working. Having tangible material to gather and examine when the time is right will help you to keep in close touch with each child's learning.

Exploring Base Ten Blocks

The Base Ten Blocks provide a spatial model of our base ten number system. The smallest blocks, cubes that measure 1 cm on a side, represent ones. These are called *units.* The long, narrow blocks that measure 10 cm by 1 cm by 1 cm represent tens. These are called *longs.* The flat, square blocks that measure 10 cm by 10 cm by 1 cm represent hundreds. These are called *flats.* The largest blocks available, cubes that measure 10 cm on a side, represent thousands. These are called *cubes.*

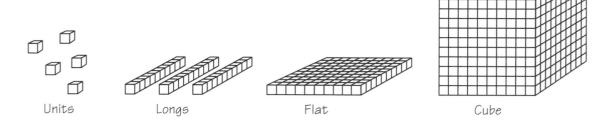

Units   Longs   Flat   Cube

The size relationships among the blocks make them ideal for the investigation of number concepts. Initially, however, children should explore independently with Base Ten Blocks before engaging in structured activities. As they move the blocks around to create designs and build structures, they may be able to discover on their own that it takes ten of a smaller block to make one of the next larger block. Children's designs and structures also lead them to employ spatial visualization and to work intuitively with the geometric concepts of shape, perimeter, area, and volume.

Base Ten Blocks are especially useful in providing children with ways to physically represent the concepts of place value and addition, subtraction, multiplication, and division of whole numbers. By building number combinations with Base Ten Blocks, children ease into the concept of regrouping, or trading, and are able to see the logical development of each operation. The blocks provide a visual foundation and understanding of the algorithms children use when doing paper-and-pencil computation. Older children can transfer their understanding of whole numbers and whole-number operations to an understanding of decimals and decimal operations.

WORKING WITH BASE TEN BLOCKS

Place-value mats, available in pads of 50, provide a means for children to organize their work as they explore the relationships among the blocks and determine how groups of blocks can be used to represent numbers. Children may begin by placing unit blocks, one at a time, in the units column on a mat. For each unit they place, they record the number corresponding to the total number of units placed (1, 2, 3, ...). They continue this process until they have accumulated 10 units, at which point they match their 10 units to 1 long and trade those units for the long, which they place in the longs column. They continue in the same way, adding units one at a time to the units column and recording the totals (11, 12, 13, ...) until it is time to trade for a second long, which they place in the longs column (20). When they finally come to 99, there are 9 units and 9 longs on the mat. Adding one more unit forces two trades: first 10 units for another long and then 10 longs for a flat (100). Then it is time to continue adding and recording units and making trades as needed as children work their way through the hundreds and up to thousands. Combining the placing and trading of longs with the act of recording the corresponding numbers provides children with a connection between concrete and symbolic representations of numbers.

Base Ten Blocks can be used to develop understanding of the meanings of addition, subtraction, multiplication, and division. Modeling addition on a place-value mat provides children with a visual basis for the concept of regrouping.

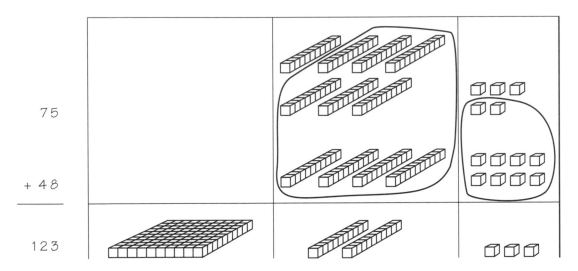

Subtraction with regrouping involves trading some of the blocks used to model the minuend of a subtraction example for smaller blocks of equal value so that the "taking away" can be accomplished. For example, in order to subtract 15 from 32, a child would trade one of the longs that represent 32 (3 longs and 2 units) for 10 units to form an equivalent representation of 32 (2 longs and 12 units). Then the child would take away 15 (1 long and 5 units) and be left with a difference of 17 (1 long and 7 units).

Multiplication can be modeled as repeated addition or with rectangular arrays. Using rectangular arrays can help in understanding the derivation of the partial products the sum of which is the total product.

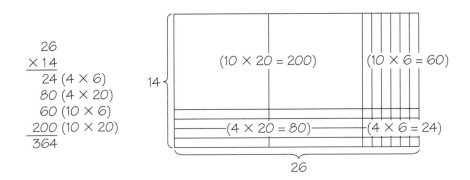

Division can be done as repeated subtraction or through building and analyzing structures and rectangular arrays.

By letting the cube, flat, long, and unit represent 1, 0.1, 0.01, and 0.001, respectively, older children can explore and develop decimal concepts, compare decimals, and perform basic operations with decimal numbers.

The squares along each face make the blocks excellent tools for visualizing and internalizing the concepts of perimeter and surface area of structures. Counting unit blocks in a structure can form the basis for understanding and finding volume.

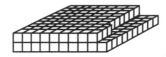

perimeter of base = 24 cm
surface area = 112 cm²
volume = 60 cm³

perimeter of base = 40 cm
surface area = 278 cm²
volume = 183 cm³

ASSESSING CHILDREN'S UNDERSTANDING

The use of Base Ten Blocks provides a perfect opportunity for authentic assessment. Watching children work with the blocks gives you a sense of how they approach a mathematical problem. Their thinking can be "seen" through their positioning of the blocks. When a class breaks up into small working groups, you are able to circulate, listen, and raise questions, all the while focusing on how individuals are thinking.

The challenges that children encounter when working with Base Ten Blocks often elicit unexpected abilities from those whose performance in more symbolic, number-oriented tasks may be weak. On the other hand, some children with good memories for numerical relationships have difficulty with spatial challenges and can more readily learn from freely exploring with Base Ten Blocks. Thus, by observing children's free exploration, you can get a sense of individual styles and intellectual strengths.

Having children describe their creations and share their strategies and thinking with the whole class gives you another opportunity for observational assessment. Furthermore, you may want to gather children's recorded work or invite them to choose pieces to add to their math portfolios.

In the beginning of the game, you have to take the highest number. In the middle of the middle and the end, you should get the lowest number. At the end you use one dice.

From: *Clear the Mat*

The person who got the most bonuses would win because you get the bones and how much you got when you rold.

From: *Ten, Ten, Ten*

Models of teachers assessing children's understanding can be found in Cuisenaire's series of videotapes listed below.

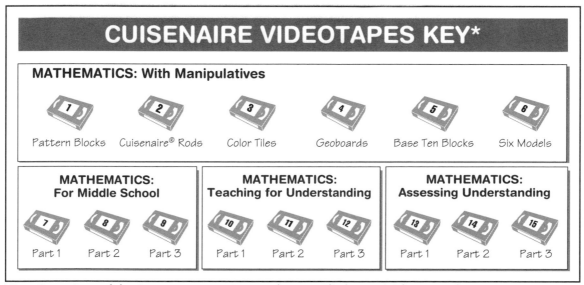

CUISENAIRE VIDEOTAPES KEY*

MATHEMATICS: With Manipulatives

1 Pattern Blocks	2 Cuisenaire® Rods	3 Color Tiles	4 Geoboards	5 Base Ten Blocks	6 Six Models

MATHEMATICS: For Middle School	MATHEMATICS: Teaching for Understanding	MATHEMATICS: Assessing Understanding
7 Part 1 8 Part 2 9 Part 3	10 Part 1 11 Part 2 12 Part 3	13 Part 1 14 Part 2 15 Part 3

*See *Overview of the Lessons,* pages 16–17, for specific lesson/video correlation.

STRANDS

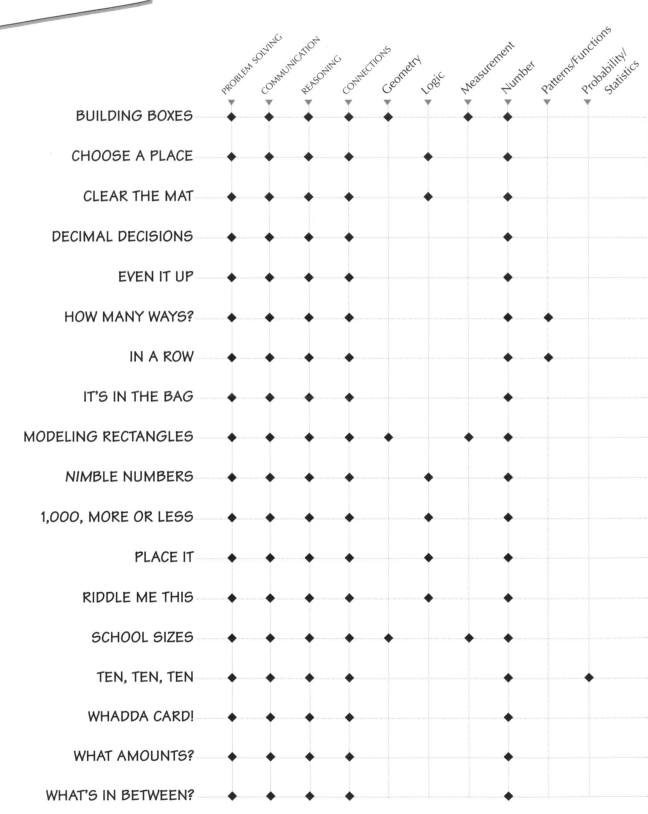

	PROBLEM SOLVING	COMMUNICATION	REASONING	CONNECTIONS	Geometry	Logic	Measurement	Number	Patterns/Functions	Probability/Statistics
BUILDING BOXES	◆	◆	◆	◆	◆		◆	◆		
CHOOSE A PLACE	◆	◆	◆	◆		◆		◆		
CLEAR THE MAT	◆	◆		◆		◆		◆		
DECIMAL DECISIONS	◆	◆	◆	◆				◆		
EVEN IT UP	◆	◆	◆	◆				◆		
HOW MANY WAYS?	◆	◆	◆	◆				◆	◆	
IN A ROW	◆	◆	◆	◆				◆	◆	
IT'S IN THE BAG	◆	◆	◆	◆				◆		
MODELING RECTANGLES	◆	◆	◆	◆	◆		◆	◆		
NIMBLE NUMBERS	◆	◆	◆	◆		◆		◆		
1,000, MORE OR LESS	◆	◆	◆	◆		◆		◆		
PLACE IT	◆	◆	◆	◆		◆		◆		
RIDDLE ME THIS	◆	◆	◆	◆		◆		◆		
SCHOOL SIZES	◆	◆	◆	◆	◆		◆	◆		
TEN, TEN, TEN	◆	◆	◆	◆				◆		◆
WHADDA CARD!	◆	◆	◆	◆						
WHAT AMOUNTS?	◆	◆	◆	◆				◆		
WHAT'S IN BETWEEN?	◆	◆	◆	◆				◆		

Correlate **THE SUPER SOURCE®** to your curriculum.

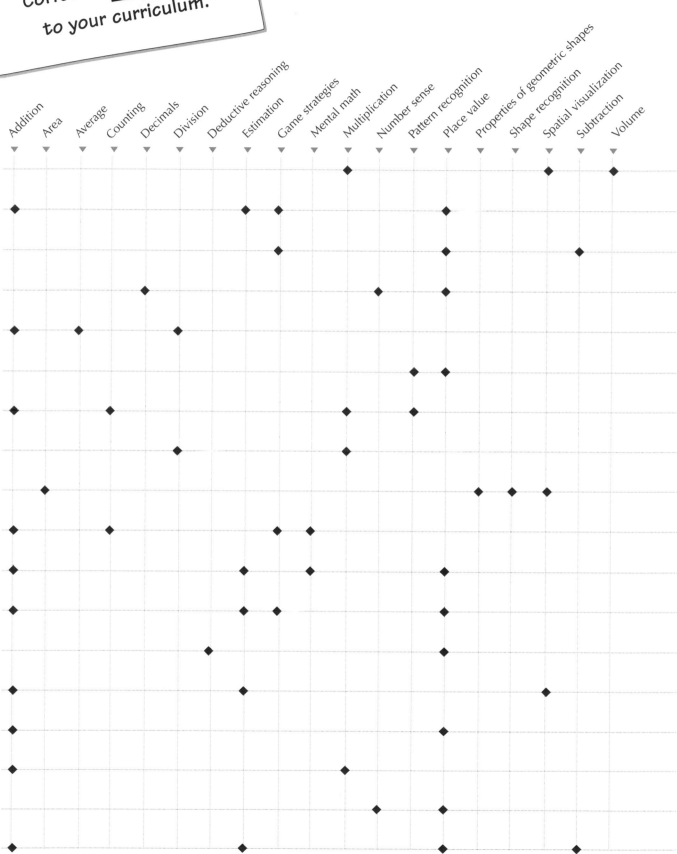

	Addition	Area	Average	Counting	Decimals	Division	Deductive reasoning	Estimation	Game strategies	Mental math	Multiplication	Number sense	Pattern recognition	Place value	Properties of geometric shapes	Shape recognition	Spatial visualization	Subtraction	Volume
											◆						◆		◆
	◆							◆	◆					◆					
									◆					◆				◆	
					◆							◆		◆					
	◆		◆			◆													
													◆	◆					
	◆			◆							◆		◆						
						◆					◆								
		◆													◆	◆	◆		
	◆			◆					◆	◆									
	◆							◆		◆				◆					
	◆							◆	◆					◆					
							◆							◆					
	◆							◆									◆		
	◆													◆					
	◆										◆								
												◆		◆					
	◆							◆						◆				◆	

Classroom-tested activities contained in these *Super Source®* Base Ten Blocks books focus on the math strands in the charts below.

THE SUPER SOURCE® Base Ten Blocks, Grades K–2

Geometry	Logic	Measurement
Number	Patterns/Functions	Probability/Statistics

THE SUPER SOURCE® Base Ten Blocks, Grades 5–6

Geometry	Logic	Measurement
Number	Patterns/Functions	Probability/Statistics

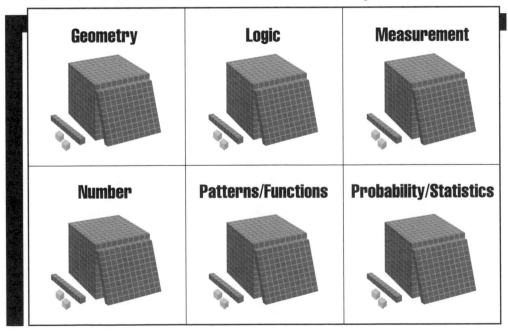

More THE SUPER SOURCE at a glance:
ADDITIONAL MANIPULATIVES for Grades 3-4

Classroom-tested activities contained in these *Super Source®* books focus on the math strands as indicated in these charts.

THE SUPER SOURCE® Snap™ Cubes, Grades 3–4

Geometry	Logic	Measurement
Number	Patterns/Functions	Probability/Statistics

THE SUPER SOURCE® Tangrams, Grades 3–4

Geometry	Logic	Measurement
Number	Patterns/Functions	Probability/Statistics

THE SUPER SOURCE® Cuisenaire® Rods, Grades 3–4

Geometry	Logic	Measurement
Number	Patterns/Functions	Probability/Statistics

THE SUPER SOURCE® Geoboards, Grades 3–4

Geometry	Logic	Measurement
Number	Patterns/Functions	Probability/Statistics

THE SUPER SOURCE® Color Tiles, Grades 3–4

Geometry	Logic	Measurement
Number	Patterns/Functions	Probability/Statistics

THE SUPER SOURCE® Pattern Blocks, Grades 3–4

Geometry	Logic	Measurement
Number	Patterns/Functions	Probability/Statistics

Overview of the Lessons

 See video key, page 11.

Base Ten Blocks, Grades 3–4

BUILDING BOXES

- Multiplication
- Volume
- Spatial visualization

Getting Ready

What You'll Need

Base Ten Blocks, 1 flat and at least 8 longs per pair

Small closed box

Overview

Children build as many different rectangular prisms as they can from eight Base Ten longs. In this activity, children have the opportunity to:

- explore volume
- discover that rectangular prisms with different dimensions can have the same volume
- use spatial reasoning

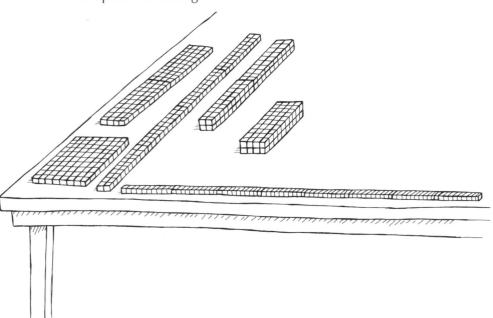

The Activity

Tell children that another name for a figure shaped like a box is rectangular prism.

You may wish to explain that the number of cubic units that make up a box is called the volume *of the box.*

Introducing

- Display a small closed box. Establish that each side of the box is a rectangle, a shape that has four square corners and the dimensions of length and width.
- Elicit that the entire box has eight square corners and the dimensions of length, width, and height.
- Hold up a flat and describe it as a kind of box. Allow children to examine the flat and give its dimensions. (Be sure they understand that the flat has a length of 10 units, a width of 10 units, and a height of 1 unit.)
- Ask children to tell how many cubes make up the flat. Accept answers that describe the flat as being made up of 100 cubes, 100 (Base Ten Blocks) units, or 100 cubic units.

On Their Own

How many different boxes can you make from the same number of Base 10 longs?

- Work with a partner. Talk about ways of making a box using Base 10 longs only.

- Now build all the different boxes you can from 8 longs. You may put the longs in 1 layer or in more than 1 layer.

- As you work, make a chart to record the length, width, and height of each box. Also record how many cubic units make up each box.

- Look for patterns in your chart.

The Bigger Picture

Thinking and Sharing

Create a class chart with the headings *Dimensions of Box* and *Cubic Units in Box* (See p. 20). Have pairs contribute their findings. Then discuss the charted data.

Use prompts like these to promote class discussion:

- How did you go about building your boxes?

- What did you do to find the length, width, and height of each box?

- Did you ever think that two boxes were different but later find out that they were really the same? Explain.

- What patterns do you see in the chart?

- How can you use the dimensions of any box to find the total number of cubic units in that box?

Writing

Ask children to describe how to find the number of cubic units that make up a Base Ten Blocks box of any size.

Extending the Activity

1. Challenge children to repeat the activity using 12 longs.

2. Ask children to use longs to build several different boxes, each with a volume of 200 cubic units.

Where's the Mathematics?

This activity provides children with a chance to informally explore volume. It also acquaints them with the concept of expressing the volume of a rectangular prism as the product of its dimensions. If you have a sufficient supply of Base Ten Blocks, provide each pair of children with more than the minimum number of 8 longs. Pairs that have access to more than 8 longs will have the advantage of not having to dismantle each box before they can build the next.

Some pairs will approach the task of building the boxes in a random fashion. Other pairs may have a more systematic approach, first building as many one-layer boxes as they can and then building two-layer boxes. They may even go on to build a four-layer box only to discover later that they had already built it, oriented differently, as a two-layer box. Children will discover that they can build six discrete boxes. They should not be surprised to find that all the boxes share the same volume—80 cubic units.

DIMENSIONS OF BOX				CUBIC UNITS IN BOX
Layers	Length	Width	Height	Volume
1	10	8	1	80
1	20	4	1	80
1	40	2	1	80
1	80	1	1	80
2	20	2	2	80
2	10	4	2	80

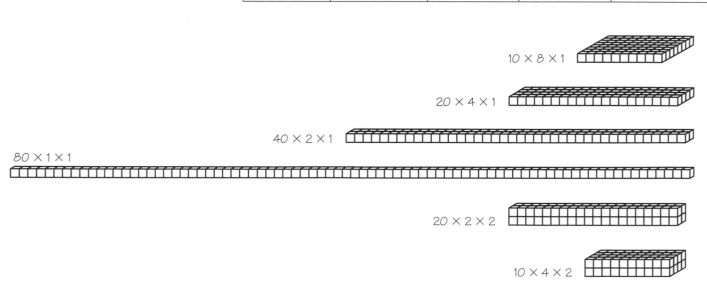

10 × 8 × 1

20 × 4 × 1

40 × 2 × 1

80 × 1 × 1

20 × 2 × 2

10 × 4 × 2

It is likely that children will record their box dimensions in various ways. Some pairs may simply list the dimensions for a particular box as, for example, "40, 2, 1." Others may be more specific by writing, for example, "The length is 40, the width is 2, and the height is 1." Still others may write "40 by 2 by 1." As you make up the class chart you may wish to record the dimensions using multiplication notation ("40 $\times$ 2 $\times$ 1") if children have not already suggested doing so.

After considering the entries in the chart above, for example, a child may say that certain dimensions, such as 4 $\times$ 20 $\times$ 1, have not yet been listed. Explain that the box represented by these dimensions is the same box represented by the dimensions 20 $\times$ 4 $\times$ 1, which has already been listed. This issue is likely to arise if children have trouble differentiating between the length and width of some of the boxes they build. Since the way in which the boxes are oriented does not matter for this activity, tell children that they may decide for themselves which dimension is the length and which is the width. (If children find this notion confusing, however, you may want to include all the ways of listing a single set of dimensions in your class chart.)

Children should conclude that each of the boxes they make with 8 longs has a volume of 80 cubic units. Some pairs will simply reason that since they have made each box from the same number of longs of equal length, the total volume of each box must be the same. They may express this mathematically by saying, for example, "Since there are 8 longs, and each has 10 units, the box must have 8 $\times$ 10, or 80 units." Other pairs may find the number of units in each layer of each box and then find the sum of the layers. They may say, for example, "This box has two layers of 40 units each. So, there are 40 plus 40, or 80 units all together." (Note that since we call the smallest Base Ten Block a unit, even though it is actually a cubic unit, allow children to express volume in terms of a total number of units, instead of as cubic units.) Insightful children may notice that multiplying the three dimensions of any box is the easiest way to find the number of (cubic) units that make up the box.

The generalizations that children make as they study the patterns generated in this activity set the stage for deriving and using formulas. If you are confident that children understand the concept of volume, you may wish to ask them to develop their own rule for finding the number of cubic units that make up a box. After children share their ideas, you may choose to present the formula for the volume of a rectangular prism, $V = l \times w \times h$, and elicit children's suggestions for how to apply it.

CHOOSE A PLACE

- Addition
- Estimation
- Place value
- Game strategies

Getting Ready

What You'll Need

Base Ten Blocks, 1 set per pair

Put-in-Place Mats, 1 per child, page 90

Number cube marked 1 to 6, 1 per group

Overhead Base Ten Blocks and/or Put-in-Place Mat transparency (optional)

Overview

In this game for two to four players, children represent each roll of a number cube with units or longs in an effort to collect Base Ten Blocks with a total value of 100. In this activity, children have the opportunity to:

- ◆ develop understanding of place value
- ◆ use addition
- ◆ develop strategic thinking skills

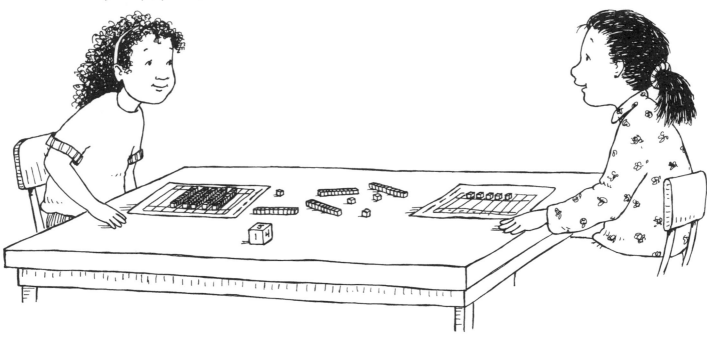

The Activity

Point out that once children have decided whether to put units or longs on their mats for a particular roll and have placed those blocks on their mat, they may not decide to make changes.

Introducing

- ◆ Display and then distribute the Put-in-Place Mats. Roll a number cube. Explain that the number you roll will tell children how many units or longs to place on their mats for a round.
- ◆ Model two sample rounds of *Choose a Place*.
- ◆ After children have placed their second number of units or longs on their mats, ask them to find the total value of their blocks.
- ◆ Lead children to talk about how they got their sums.

On Their Own

Play Choose a Place!

Here are the rules.

1. This is a game for 2 to 4 players. The object is to collect Base 10 Blocks with a total value closest to 100 without going over 100. Players decide who will be first.

2. To begin a round, a player rolls a number cube and says the number rolled.

3. Each player decides whether to place that number of units or that number of longs on a mat that looks like this.

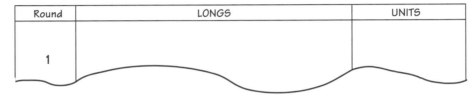

4. Players take turns rolling the number cube and putting either units or longs on their mats.

5. After 5 rounds, players figure out their scores. They do this by finding the sum of the values of their blocks, trading if they need to.

6. Players record their totals for the game. Whoever gets the total that is closest to 100 without going over is the winner.

- Play 5 games of *Choose a Place*.

- Be ready to talk about good moves and bad moves.

The Bigger Picture

Thinking and Sharing

Invite children to talk about their games and describe some of the thinking they did.

Use prompts like these to promote class discussion:

- On each turn, how did you decide whether to put down units or longs?

- Were you ever sorry about the choice you made on a turn? Explain.

- How did you decide whose sum was closest to 100?

- Were there any scores that went over 100? Were any of these closer to 100 than the winning score? Explain.

- What did you find out from playing this game?

Writing

Have children record the numbers they rolled for one game and the value of the blocks they put down for each roll. Suggest that they examine this data and describe how, if they could have changed one move or another, they would have gotten closer to 100.

Extending the Activity

1. Have children play *Choose a Place* so that the winner is the one whose total is closest to 100 even if it goes over 100.

Teacher Talk

Where's the Mathematics?

Playing this game helps children develop their understanding of the structure of the base ten number system. Children become able to link their concrete work with blocks to the more abstract notion of place value and the algorithm for addition with regrouping. After playing individually several times, children might want to play as pairs—one member of each pair manipulating the blocks and the other member recording the five addends and finding the sum of their values.

When children begin to play *Choose a Place,* they are likely not to think about strategies as they place blocks on their mats. For each round they may merely take longs or units at random. Some children may begin to strategize by picking only longs for the first few rounds of a game (in hopes of quickly getting a sum of 80 or 90) and then picking only units for the last round or two. Other children may think that by picking only units throughout the game they will be protected from going beyond 100, unaware at first of how far from 100 that strategy will leave them after five rounds. Still other children become so focused on accumulating 10 longs that they forget about the units they have collected altogether. They may think that they've won the game only to realize that their unit blocks will take them beyond 100. For example, throughout the game shown at right, player B had been keeping an eye on her longs column only. She was pleased to have gotten a total of 10 longs; that is, until she realized that she had forgotten all about her units!

2. Have children play the game using a 4–9 number cube. With this cube, children should try for a total of *200* without going over.

3. Extend the Put-in-Place Mat by adding a "Flats" column to the left of the "Longs" column. Copy and distribute these three-places mats for children's use in playing the game again. This time, have them first choose a target number between 700 and 1,000. For each roll of the number cube, children should decide whether to put down units, longs, or flats. Again, whoever gets closest to the target number without going over is the winner.

Player A
PUT-IN-PLACE MAT

Round	LONGS	UNITS
1		
2		
3		
4		
5		
	TOTAL →	84

Digits Rolled
5
5
3
6
2

Player B
PUT-IN-PLACE MAT

Round	LONGS	UNITS
1		
2		
3		
4		
5		
	TOTAL →	100-NO it's ||| !

Upon reviewing their own recordings of lost games, children usually determine that if they had chosen a different place for one move or another they could have come closer to winning. Ideally then, as they play, children begin to use their experiences with previous games and start to estimate their totals at the end of each round to help them better make their choices for subsequent rounds. Children will then intuitively begin to use probability to guide their choices of blocks as they apply their strategies for getting close to 100.

CLEAR THE MAT

- • Place value
- • Subtraction
- • Game strategies

Getting Ready

What You'll Need

Base Ten Blocks, 1 set per pair

Base Ten Blocks Place Value Mat,
1 per pair

Number cubes marked 1 to 6,
2 per pair

Overhead Base Ten Blocks (optional)

Overview

In this game for teams of two, children roll a number cube to determine the value of the Base Ten Blocks to remove from their place-value mats. They look for a strategy for being the first team to remove all the blocks from their mat. In this activity, children have the opportunity to:

- ◆ use estimation skills
- ◆ use subtraction
- ◆ develop strategic thinking skills

The Activity

Introducing

- ◆ Show children a place-value mat with 1 flat in the "flats" (hundreds) column. Elicit that the flat represents 1 hundred, or 100 units.
- ◆ Ask a volunteer to write any 2-digit number on the chalkboard.
- ◆ Tell children to think about how they can take blocks equal in value to that number from the flat on the mat.
- ◆ Establish that, in order to subtract, they would have to trade—1 flat for 10 longs—then, if necessary, 1 long for 10 units.
- ◆ Have someone do the trading, taking away the blocks for the 2-digit number and then announcing the difference, or how much of the hundred is left.
- ◆ Record the action by writing the corresponding subtraction example on the board.

On Their Own

Play *Clear the Mat!*

Here are the rules.

1. This is a game for 2 to 4 teams of 2 players each. The object is to be the first team to remove all the blocks from its place-value mat.

2. Each team starts with 3 flats on its mat.

3. Teams take turns rolling the number cubes and using the numbers rolled to make a 2-digit number. (For example, a team that rolls a 3 and a 5 could make either 35 or 53.) One team member says the number and takes blocks with that value off the mat. The other team member writes the subtraction. The other teams help check their work.

4. A team loses a turn if:

   ◆ it makes a mistake subtracting.

   ◆ each of the numbers it can make is greater than the value of the blocks left on its mat.

5. On any turn, if a team decides to subtract just a few blocks it may choose to roll just one number cube.

6. Play continues until 1 team rolls the exact amount left on its mat. Then it clears its mat...and wins the game!

- Play several games of *Clear the Mat*.
- Look for winning strategies.

The Bigger Picture

Thinking and Sharing

Invite children to talk about their games and describe some of the thinking they did.

Use prompts like these to promote class discussion:

- ◆ On each roll, how did you decide which 2-digit number to make?
- ◆ What kind of trading did you have to do in order to subtract?
- ◆ Which subtractions were the easiest to do? Explain.
- ◆ What was the greatest number you could subtract on any one turn? What was the least number?
- ◆ Did you ever decide to roll just one die? Was that a good decision? Why?
- ◆ What is a strategy for winning this game?
- ◆ As the game went on, did you ever change your strategy? If so, tell how.

Writing

Have children turn one of the subtraction examples they recorded during the game into a story problem.

Teacher Talk

Where's the Mathematics?

This activity gives children subtraction practice while it engages them in developing and analyzing game strategies. Many children will begin playing with no particular strategy in mind. They may develop a strategy that they continue to use throughout the game, or they may develop one that they adjust as the game progresses.

Children will come to realize that the greater the number they make on each turn, the faster they will come close to clearing their mats. But they will have to re-evaluate this strategy once they are left with blocks having a value of 66 or less. At that point, a team could lose its turn for rolling a number that is greater than the value of the blocks that remain on its mat.

One team may keep on rolling both cubes until it loses a turn for rolling a number greater than the amount left on its mat. To be sure of not losing a turn, another team may develop the strategy of rolling only one cube once it is left with a blocks of a certain value. Such a team may, for example, decide that, once its blocks are worth 40, its chances of rolling numbers greater than 40 increase. And so, once it reaches 40, it may choose to use just one number cube to keep from rolling numbers that are too high. Conservative players may decide to start rolling just one cube as soon as their block values go below 66. As children play the game several times, they will refine their strategies.

Manipulating Base Ten Blocks in this way helps children to better under-stand the standard subtraction algorithm. Children first go through the pro-cedure of finding a difference by using the manipulatives and then connect the procedure to the written symbols that are used to record it. Some teams may decide to have one player manipulate the blocks while another player does the paper-and-pencil computation, followed by teammates verifying their answers together.

After trading a flat for longs, children may begin to remove blocks working from left to right, subtracting the requisite number of longs first and then the

Extending the Activity

1. Have teams play *Clear the Mat* again, this time starting with a thousands cube on each mat and rolling either one, two, or three number cubes on a turn.

2. Have teams play *Fill the Mat,* a version of this game based on addition instead of subtraction. Teams start the game with empty mats. They take turns rolling the number cubes and adding blocks to their mat in an effort to be the first to fill their mat with blocks having a total value of 300.

number of units. (This, as opposed to the way in which we typically record subtraction, working from right to left—first subtracting ones, then subtracting tens.) Whether they remove blocks from left to right or from right to left, children should be able to describe their actions and match them to the way they recorded the subtraction. Here is the way one child described what she recorded after her team began the game by rolling 6 and 4, which it used as the number 46.

> I started by writing "300 – 46." After we traded 1 flat for 10 longs, I crossed out the 3 in the hundreds place and wrote "2," which means two hundred. Then I crossed out the zero in the tens place and wrote "10" to mean 10 tens.
>
> After we traded 1 long for 10 units, I crossed out the 10 in the tens place and wrote "9" to show that 9 tens were left. I crossed out the 0 in the ones place and wrote "10" to mean 10 ones.
>
> Then we took 6 units off the mat. There were 4 units left so I wrote "4" in the ones place below the line. We took 4 longs away from the 9, which left 5, so I wrote "5" in the tens place below the line.
>
> There were 2 flats left on the mat, so I wrote "2" in the hundreds place below the line. So, the blocks we had left on our mat were worth 254.

$$
\begin{array}{r}
\overset{\overset{9\ 10}{2\ \cancel{10}}}{\cancel{300}} \\
-\ 46 \\
\hline
254
\end{array}
$$

Although children may play this game individually, having them play in teams of two encourages them to communicate mathematically as they discuss the subtraction process along with possible strategies for winning.

DECIMAL DECISIONS

Getting Ready

What You'll Need

Base Ten Blocks, 1 set per pair

Number cubes marked 1 to 6,
1 per pair

Overview

Children use Base Ten Blocks to model a "major decimal." Then they decide how to model a "minor decimal," a decimal whose value is less than that of the major decimal. In this activity, children have the opportunity to:

◆ develop an understanding of decimal place value

◆ model decimal amounts

◆ compare the relative values of tenths and hundredths

◆ add decimal amounts

The Activity

You may wish to introduce (or review) the use of the symbols for less than (<) and greater than (>) and have children write a few number sentences using these symbols to show how the numbers compare.

Introducing

◆ Display a Base Ten flat and have children do the same.

◆ Tell children to cover their flat with longs. Acknowledge that 10 longs are needed to completely cover 1 flat.

◆ Elicit that if a flat has the value of one whole, or 1, then each long has the value of one tenth ($\frac{1}{10}$) of 1.

◆ Write 0.1 on the board and explain that this is the decimal form of the fraction one tenth.

◆ Then write 0.3. Tell children to use their blocks to show three tenths.

◆ Display a Base Ten unit and ask how many units would be needed to cover 1 flat. Acknowledge that 100 units would be needed.

◆ Elicit that if a flat has the value of 1, then each unit has the value of one hundredth ($\frac{1}{100}$) of 1.

◆ Write 0.01 on the board. Explain that this is the way to write the fraction one hundredth as a decimal.

◆ Now write 0.14. Challenge children to use their blocks to show 14 hundredths.

◆ Establish that there are two ways to do this—with 1 long and 4 units and with 14 units.

On Their Own

How can you use Base 10 Blocks to show a decimal that is worth less than a "major decimal"?

- Work with a partner. Put a flat between you. Your flat has the value of 1.

- Whoever goes first models a *major decimal*. Here's how:

  - Roll a number cube. Take longs to match the number rolled. Record the value of the longs as a number of tenths.

  - Roll again. Take units for this roll. Record their value as hundredths.

  - Push the blocks together. Find the sum they represent. Write the sum in decimal form. (This is your major decimal.)

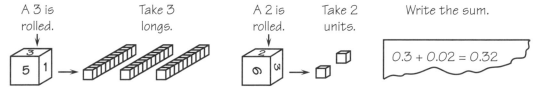

| A 3 is rolled. | Take 3 longs. | A 2 is rolled. | Take 2 units. | Write the sum. |

$$0.3 + 0.02 = 0.32$$

- Whoever goes second models a *minor decimal* this way:

  - Roll the number cube. What digit did you roll? Model it with longs (tenths) or units (hundredths) or with both longs and units. You must represent a sum whose value is *less than* the value of the major decimal.

  - Record the value of your minor decimal.

0.06

- Write a number sentence that compares the 2 decimals.

0.32 > 0.06

- Repeat the activity several times. Take turns going first.

The Bigger Picture

Thinking and Sharing

Invite children to identify their major decimals and to tell how they modeled their minor decimals. Have pairs share the number sentences they wrote to compare the decimals.

Use prompts like these to promote class discussion:

- What is the greatest major decimal you can model? the least?
- How did you figure out the value of your major decimal?
- How did you model your minor decimal?
- Were you always able to model a minor decimal? Explain.
- How did you compare your decimals? How else could you compare?

Extending the Activity

1. Have children do the activity two more times, but instead of having them compare each pair of major and minor decimals, have them record and order the four decimals they model, from least to greatest.

Teacher Talk

Where's the Mathematics?

Children will determine the values of their major decimals in different ways. Some may count the tenths and the hundredths and then record them separately as, for example, 3 tenths and 4 hundredths. Children who record the sum of the amounts correctly in decimal notation, for example 0.34, may be helped to see certain decimal relationships—in this case, that 3 tenths and 4 hundredths is equivalent to 34 hundredths.

Before children begin the activity, you may wish to tell them that when they have their major decimals they should read them aloud to you. This will give you the chance to see if children understand that they must now model a decimal whose value is less than that of their major decimal. You will find that some children will record their first and second rolls in fraction form as, for example, $\frac{3}{10}$ and $\frac{4}{100}$. Remind such children how to add the two fractions by using the common denominator 100. Be sure they understand that they must then add $\frac{30}{100}$ and $\frac{4}{100}$ to get the sum $\frac{34}{100}$.

Children should realize that because 6 is the highest digit that can be rolled on a 1-to-6 number cube, the greatest major decimal that can be modeled is 0.66. Similarly, because 1 is the lowest digit that can be rolled, the least major decimal that can be modeled is 0.11.

Children may set about deciding on which Base Ten Blocks to use for the minor decimal in a variety of ways. Some may approach the task randomly, choosing any combination of longs and units that matches the number rolled. Others may not be sure of whether the minor decimal they model is, in fact, less than the major decimal until they actually select the blocks and count them. For example, if the major decimal is 0.42, a child who rolls a 6 for the minor decimal might off-handedly take 5 longs and 1 unit and then realize that these blocks would model the decimal 0.51, which is greater than the major decimal. Still other children may see the need for finding a system that will help them to be sure of modeling a decimal whose value is less than that of the major decimal. One system might be to start with the number of longs that is one less than the number of longs used for the major

2. Have children repeat the activity, but this time have them model a minor decimal whose value is *greater than* that of the major decimal.

---

decimal and then to take as many units as necessary to make up the total number rolled. So, a child who rolls a 4 for the minor decimal (when the major decimal is 0.42) would take 3 longs and 1 unit to model 0.31.

In order to avoid confusion, some children may opt to use units alone to model their minor decimals. For the example above, these children would simply take 4 units to model the minor decimal four hundredths (0.04). Encourage any children who continue to use this method to sometimes use a combination of longs and units to model their minor decimals.

Children may use different recording methods to compare their major and minor decimals. Some children may use words only, writing for example, "31 hundredths is less than 42 hundredths" or "42 hundredths is greater than 31 hundredths." Others may use symbols only, writing for example, "0.31 < 0.42" or "0.42 > 0.31." (Because of the way the activity is worded, it is more likely that children will write less-than sentences rather than greater-than sentences.)

Children who attempt to repeat the activity by modeling minor decimals that are *greater than* the major decimals should conclude that they cannot succeed at this using only longs and units. You may wish to allow children who are ready to work with mixed decimals (which have both whole-number parts and decimal parts) to use flats, as well as longs and units, in order to make these "greater-than" minor decimals.

This activity enables children to understand decimal concepts by helping them to develop visual images of tenths and hundredths. You may want to make this activity available at a math center so that children can return to it from time to time. Having children repeat the activity by replacing the 1-to-6 number cube with a 4-to-9 number cube or with a spinner labeled 0 to 9 or a decahedron die labeled 0 to 9 will give children the opportunity to explore additional decimal amounts.

EVEN IT UP

Getting Ready

What You'll Need

Base Ten Blocks, 1 set per group

Small paper bags—some, marked Longs, should contain three slips of paper marked 1, 2, and 3; others, marked Units, should contain nine slips of paper marked 1–9, 1 of each bag per group

Overhead Base Ten Blocks (optional)

Overview

Children pick slips of paper that indicate which two-digit numbers to model with Base Ten Blocks. Then they work in a group to figure out ways to share all their blocks equally. In this activity, children have the opportunity to:

- view division as making equal shares
- develop an understanding of the meaning of average

The Activity

Introducing

- Display a row of 6 units. Form another row of blocks by placing 1 long below the units, aligning the rows at one end. Have children copy this.

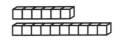

- Ask children how they can make the two rows equal in number.

- Elicit that one way to start is by trading the long for 10 units.

- Have children share their strategies for "evening up" the rows.

- After children have made two rows of 8 units, explain that by making the rows equal, they are showing that 8 is the *average* of 6 and 10.

- Tell children to rearrange their 16 units into two rows again—this time into a row of 12 and a row of 4. Then ask them to find the number that is the average of 12 and 4.

- Discuss why it is possible for one number to be the average of more than one set of numbers.

On Their Own

> **How can you share Base 10 Blocks equally so that everyone has blocks with the same value?**
>
> - Work in a group of 3. Get a bag marked "Longs" and a bag marked "Units."
> - Take turns picking. When it is your turn, here's what to do:
>   - Pick 1 slip of paper from the Longs bag. Take blocks for that many longs.
>   - Return the slip to the Longs bag.
>
>   Then,
>   - Pick a slip from the Units bag. Take blocks for that many units.
>   - Return the slip to the Units bag.
> - Find the value of the blocks you picked. Write down the number.
> - Have everyone show their blocks and tell their number.
> - Find a way to share all the blocks that everyone picked so that you each get blocks with the same value. Decide on a way to record what you did.
> - Now, do the activity again. This time, work in a group of 4 or 5!

The Bigger Picture

Thinking and Sharing

Have volunteers discuss their methods of making the equal shares of blocks. Ask several groups to list the numbers they started with, the total value of their blocks, and the value of each share (the average). Compile their findings in a class chart like this one.

	Value of Numbers Picked	Total Value of Each Group's Blocks	Value of Each Share (Average)
Sue	12		
Robert	18	51	17
Lee	21		

Use prompts like these to promote class discussion:

- What number did each person in your group start with?
- How did you go about finding the equal shares?
- Did you have to make trades? Did you rearrange the blocks in some other way? Explain.
- If you had blocks that you couldn't share three ways, what did you do? How do you think the extras would affect the average?
- What number was the average of the three numbers your group picked? Do you

Writing

Tell children to pretend that a friend has asked them to feed his pet monkey while he is away for four weeks. The friend said, "The monkey eats an average of 15 bananas a week." Have children decide how many bananas the monkey might eat for each of the four weeks. Then ask them to explain their thinking.

Teacher Talk

Where's the Mathematics?

Even It Up gives children the chance to explore ways to divide an amount into equal shares to determine the meaning of *average*. Children work with division, with and without remainders, as they share a collection of Base Ten Blocks among the members of their group. Use the activity to introduce the concept of average or to reinforce what children already know.

Groups are likely to take different approaches to sharing the blocks three

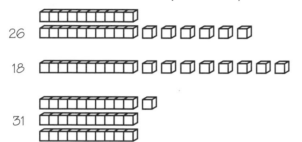

ways. Some groups might use a compensation method in which they line up the amounts, one below the other (much as they did in the *Introducing* activity), and then trade as necessary, moving the blocks from one row to another to even up the shares. For example, assume that the three members of a group started with shares of 26, 18, and 31, aligning the blocks as shown at left.

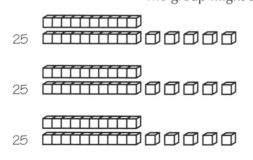

The group might take 1 long from the 31 and put it with the 18. This would leave each share with 2 longs. They might then move 3 units from what was 18 to what was 31 and then take 1 unit from the 26 and put it with what was 31. Thus, they would be creating equal shares, each with 2 longs and 5 units, for an average of 25.

Children can evaluate the reasonableness of their results by noticing that the average of a group of numbers must fall somewhere between the extremes of those numbers. They would realize, for example, that the average of 26, 18, and 31 must be greater than 18 and less than 31. An "average" of less than 18 or more than 31 would not make sense.

Another approach that children might take is to first combine all the group's blocks and then begin dividing them equally among the members of the group. Children may put all their blocks together in a pile in the middle of the table and then, in turn, each take one long, then another long, if there

Extending the Activity

Have children refer back to the numbers they picked the last time they did the activity. Tell them to add 2 more units to each of their starting numbers and then predict how these additions might affect the average. Direct children to repeat the activity with these larger numbers and then compare their outcomes to their predictions.

---

are enough to go around, until there are no more left. Then children may each take units, one at a time, until there are no more of these left. Have children explain what they did if they had longs left over (traded them for units) or if they had units left over (set them aside).

Have children share their methods for recording how they found the average. You may choose to introduce the paper-and-pencil procedure for finding the average—finding the sum of the addends and then dividing that sum by the number of addends—by explaining that combining all the blocks is like finding the sum of the numbers they represent. Then sharing all the blocks equally is like dividing the sum by the number of addends (the number of people in the group). Demonstrate this by working out an example of this on the chalkboard using one group's data.

As they write about the possible numbers of bananas that the monkey might eat, based on the average of 15 a week, some children will say that the monkey might eat 15 bananas during each of the four weeks. While this is a legitimate response, do not leave children with this suggestion alone, lest they mistakenly infer that an average is necessarily the same number as each of the addends on which it is based. Point out that there are many other possibilities. Some children may offer amounts of bananas, none of which is 15, for each of the four weeks. They may say, for example, that the monkey might eat 16 bananas the first week, 14 the second week, 17 the third week, and 13 the fourth week. If no one asks how it is possible for none of the weeks to contain the number that is the average, be sure to raise this question for discussion.

Once children understand the sharing of Base Ten Blocks as a means of finding averages and/or once they fully understand the paper-and-pencil method of finding averages, you may wish to have them use the calculator to verify their work. Be sure that children know to key in each of their starting numbers (addends) and to press the addition key between entries. Then have them press the equals key to find the sum of the addends, press the division key, press the key that represents the number of addends, and finally press the equals key to find the average of the addends.

HOW MANY WAYS?

• Place value
• Pattern recognition

Getting Ready

What You'll Need

Base Ten Blocks, 1 set per group

Base Ten Blocks Place-Value Mat, 1 per group

Overhead Base Ten Blocks (optional)

Overview

Children search to find all the possible combinations of Base Ten Blocks that can be used to represent a number. In this activity, children have the opportunity to:

◆ develop understanding of place value

◆ look for patterns

◆ organize information

The Activity

Introducing

◆ Ask children to model the number 52 using the least number of Base Ten Blocks possible.

◆ Discuss children's models. Elicit that 5 longs and 2 units is the least number of blocks that can be used.

◆ Ask children how they could model 52 using the greatest possible number of Base Ten Blocks. Establish that 52 units would be needed.

◆ Call on volunteers to show the number 52 in still other ways.

◆ Have children share all the different ways they find.

On Their Own

How many different ways can you use Base 10 Blocks to model a number?

- Work with a group. Use Base 10 Blocks to show the number 123.

- Now use blocks to show 123 another way.

- Try to find more different ways to model 123 with blocks until you agree that you have found every possible way.

- Decide on how to organize and record your data.

- Look for patterns in your data.

- Be ready to talk about any patterns you find.

The Bigger Picture

Thinking and Sharing

Ask volunteers to share their models and their recording methods. Help children generate a class chart to show all the ways they found to show 123. You may wish to set up a chart like this one and have groups contribute their data.

Flats	Longs	Units
1	2	3
1	1	13
1	0	23
0	12	3

Use prompts like these to promote class discussion:

- How did you decide which blocks to use to show 123?

- What was the least number of blocks you used? What was the greatest number of blocks?

- Do you think that you could find even more ways to show 123 if you had more blocks? Explain.

- How did you organize your findings?

- How did you record your findings?

- Did you discover any patterns? If so, what are they?

Writing

Ask children to explain whether they think they would be able to find more ways to model the number 100 or more ways to model the number 165 using Base Ten Blocks.

Extending the Activity

1. Have children find and record all the different ways they could pay for something that costs $1.20 if they had dollar bills, dimes, and pennies.

Where's the Mathematics?

This activity gives children the opportunity to explore place value and to develop an understanding of how to trade between places. Recognizing that there are many different ways to represent a single number is valuable preparation for further work with arithmetical operations.

Children may approach the task of representing the number in a variety of ways. Some groups will begin by randomly finding different combinations of blocks and then begin to notice patterns and explore them. Other groups will work systematically, first replacing the 1 flat with 10 longs and then replacing each long with 10 units, as necessary, exchanging and adjusting the numbers of longs and units with each trade.

A variety of recording systems may emerge. Some groups will chart their findings, others will draw pictures, and still others will write sentences.

This chart shows all 16 combinations of Base Ten Blocks that can be used to model the number 123.

Flats	Longs	Units
1	2	3
1	1	13
1	0	23
0	12	3
0	11	13
0	10	23
0	9	33
0	8	43
0	7	53
0	6	63
0	5	73
0	4	83
0	3	93
0	2	103
0	1	113
0	0	123

In order to discover all the ways of modeling 123, each group will need a minimum of 1 flat, 12 longs, and 123 units. If such quantities are not available, have children find as many combinations as they can with the blocks

2. Challenge children to develop a rule for finding the total number of possible ways to model any three-digit number from 100 to 199 using Base Ten Blocks.

---

they have and then ask them if they think that there may be more possible ways. By organizing what they have worked out and recording it in chart form, children can discover patterns and extend them to find any ways that they may have missed.

When asked about whether or not they discovered patterns, children may look at the chart above and point out, for example, that as the number of longs decreases by 1 the number of units increases by 10. If asked to explain this, children may say that it is because 10 units have the same value as 1 long.

Children can simulate many shopping problems using Base Ten Blocks to find the different ways to pay for something that costs $1.20. Help them establish that they can work out the problem with blocks by using flats to represent dollars, longs to represent dimes, and units to represent pennies.

It would help children to formulate a rule for finding the total number of ways they can model a three-digit number with 1 in the hundreds place by repeating the activity several times, each time modeling a different number. You may wish to suggest that they do this using the numbers 100, 145, and/or 179. (A few children may notice that the digits in the hundreds and tens places determine how many times they can regroup to show the number another way.) The rule can be broken down into three steps, as follows:

1. Add 1 to the digit in the tens place.
2. Add 1 to the number represented by the two digits in the hundreds and tens places.
3. Add the two totals. The sum is equal to the number of ways that the original number can be modeled.

The chart below shows how, by following the steps above, it can be proven that there are 16 ways of showing 123 and that there are 12 ways of showing 100, 20 ways of showing 145, and 26 ways of showing 179.

123	100	145	179
2 + 1 = 3	0 + 1 = 1	4 + 1 = 5	7 + 1 = 8
12 + 1 = 13	10 + 1 = 11	14 + 1 = 15	17 + 1 = 18
3 + 13 = **16**	1 + 11 = **12**	5 + 15 = **20**	8 + 18 = **26**

IN A ROW

- • Pattern recognition
- • Counting
- • Addition
- • Multiplication

Getting Ready

What You'll Need

Base Ten Blocks, 1 set per pair

Base Ten Block Grid Paper, 1 sheet per child, page 96

Overhead Base Ten Blocks (optional)

Overview

Children use Base Ten Blocks to extend a given pattern, to create their own pattern, and to find the total value of each pattern. In this activity, children have the opportunity to:

- ◆ discover patterns
- ◆ use patterns to make predictions
- ◆ use patterns to make generalizations

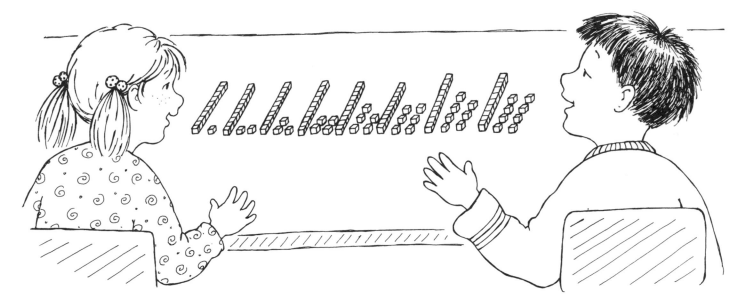

The Activity

Introducing

- ◆ Display this pattern of longs and units and have children copy it.
- ◆ Explain that these are the first four terms of a six-term pattern.
- ◆ Point out that the fifth term is what comes next in this pattern and that the sixth term will complete the pattern.
- ◆ Have volunteers explain how they could predict what the sixth, or last, term would be.
- ◆ Explain that the *value* of the pattern is the sum of the values of all the terms.
- ◆ Invite children to share ways of finding the value of this pattern.

On Their Own

How can you use Base 10 Blocks to extend a pattern and then find its value?

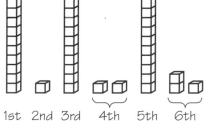

1st 2nd 3rd 4th 5th 6th

- Work with a partner. Here are the first 6 terms of a 16-term pattern. Talk about them.

- Predict what the 16th term of this pattern would be. (See if you can figure it out without extending the pattern.)

- Now use blocks to extend the pattern through the 16th term.

- Figure out ways to find the value of this 16-term pattern. Then find the value. Record your work.

- Design your own pattern using Base 10 Blocks! Stop after the 6th term.

- Predict the 16th term of your pattern.

- Use blocks to extend your pattern and find its value.

- Be ready to talk about what you did and what you found out.

The Bigger Picture

Thinking and Sharing

Ask children to share how they predicted the 16th term of the given pattern. Then have them describe how they created their own block patterns.

Use prompts like these to promote class discussion:

- How did you decide on the next terms in the pattern?

- Was your prediction of the 16th term correct? If not, was it close? Explain.

- Was it easier to complete the given pattern or to design your own pattern? Why?

- Were you able to find the value of a pattern through the 16th term without actually building each of the 16 terms? Explain.

Drawing and Writing

Allow children to choose manipulatives other than Base Ten Blocks with which to build a pattern. They may choose from Color Tiles, Cuisenaire® Rods, Pattern Blocks, Snap™ Cubes, or any other manipulatives with multiple attributes. After children create their pattern, have them describe it in words, drawing and annotating it, if possible.

Extending the Activity

1. Have children find the value of this pattern through the 12th term.

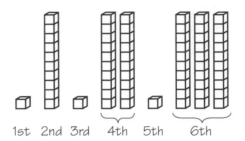

1st 2nd 3rd 4th 5th 6th

Teacher Talk

Where's the Mathematics?

Patterning helps children to understand that there is a logic and order to mathematics. A child who has experience in patterning will know how to facilitate the problem-solving strategy "Look for a Pattern" to analyze and solve story problems. Number patterns, such as those that can be found on the hundreds chart, are familiar to children. In order to grow mathematically, however, children must have experience using and building a variety of different kinds of patterns.

Children may not successfully predict the 16th term of the given pattern. They may not even come close. Their predictions are likely to depend on their experience in interpreting number patterns and in working with Base Ten Blocks. Later, as children begin to extend the pattern, they may change their predictions. Reconsidering a prediction after finding additional data is a valuable skill for building number sense.

Some children may look at the given pattern merely as an arrangement of blocks in which 1 long separates two groups of units that increase in number sequentially by one. They may find the value of the pattern by first finding the value of the 8 longs and then adding to that the sum of the eight groups of units. That is, children may determine the value, 116, by:

1. counting the longs and finding their value (8 longs = 80).
2. adding to find the value of the sequential groups of units
   $(1 + 2 + 3... + 8 = 36)$.
3. finding the total value of the longs and the units $(80 + 36 = 116)$.

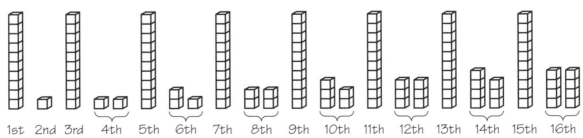

1st 2nd 3rd 4th 5th 6th 7th 8th 9th 10th 11th 12th 13th 14th 15th 16th

---

2. Challenge children to find the value of this pattern through the 8th term.

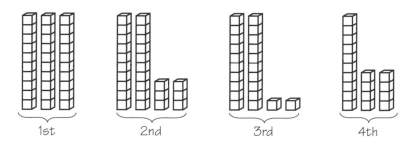

1st   2nd   3rd   4th

Other children may view the pattern as a grouping of consecutive numbers, each represented by 1 long and 1 more unit than the last. That is, they may see a pattern in which the first and second terms have the combined value of 11, the third and fourth terms have a combined value of 12, the fifth and sixth terms a value of 13, and so on. It follows, then, that to determine the value of the 16-term pattern seen in this way, children need to find the sum of just eight amounts: 11 + 12 + 13 + 14 + 15 + 16 + 17 + 18 = *116*.

Children with patterning experience may notice patterns within the given pattern! They will notice that each odd-numbered term is a 10 and that the even-numbered terms are the consecutive counting numbers. If they notice that the number of units in any even-numbered term is equal to half of the number of that term, they will readily determine that the 16th term will be equal to half of 16, or 8 units.

Once children understand how to determine the value of the 16-term pattern, they should have no trouble finding the 7th through 12th terms of a new pattern (first pattern in *Extending the Activity*) and then finding the value of this 12-term pattern. They should notice that the odd-numbered terms each have a value of 1, for a total of 6, and that the even-numbered terms represent the consecutive multiples of 10, for a total of 210. So, the value of the 12-term pattern is 6 + 210, or 216.

Finding the value of the 8-term pattern (second pattern in *Extending the Activity*) will actually present little challenge once children realize that the 2nd term has a value that is 4 less than that of the 1st term. The 3rd term is 4 less than the 2nd term, the 4th is 4 less than the 3rd term, and so on. Counting backwards by 4s from 30 in this way means that the 8th term has a value of 2. So, the value of the 8-term pattern is 30 + 26 + 22 + 18 + 14 + 10 + 6 + 2, or 128.

IT'S IN THE BAG

Getting Ready

What You'll Need

Base Ten Blocks, 1 set per group

Small paper bags, each marked with a letter and filled with a collection of flats and longs representing an amount such as 15, 18, 20, 24, 25, 26, 27, 28, 30, and 36, 1 per group

Overhead Base Ten Blocks (optional)

Overview

Children work in a group to determine whether or not a collection of Base Ten Blocks can be shared equally among them with no remainders. In this activity, children have the opportunity to:

◆ view division as making equal shares

◆ predict outcomes

◆ look for patterns in division problems

◆ discover that multiplication is the inverse of division

The Activity

Introducing

◆ Display 1 long and 2 units. Establish that the value of these blocks is 12.

◆ Call on *two* volunteers. Ask them what they can do to share the blocks so that they each get blocks of equal value.

◆ After children show how to trade the long for 10 units, they should distribute the 12 units equally so that they each have 6.

◆ Take the 6 units back from each child and say that you are going to "trade the blocks back" for the long and 2 units.

◆ Now ask *five* volunteers to show how they can share one long and 2 units equally. After they make five shares of two, acknowledge that 2 extra units remain. These are the "leftovers."

On Their Own

> **When you make equal shares of Base 10 Blocks, will there be any leftovers?**
>
> - Work with a group of 5. Get a bag of Base 10 Blocks. Spill the blocks from the bag.
>
> - Find the value of the blocks. Record the letter of the bag and the total value of the blocks.
>
> - Predict whether or not 2 of you can share the blocks equally with no leftovers.
>
> - Two of you should share the blocks equally. Record how many blocks each of you gets. Record the number of leftovers, if any.
>
> - Put all the blocks together again.
>
> - Now share the same blocks equally among 3 of you, then among 4 of you, then among 5 of you. Each time, first predict whether or not there will be leftovers. Then share and record your findings.
>
> - Return all the blocks to the bag. Close the bag.
>
> - Trade bags with another group. Repeat the activity using your new bag.

The Bigger Picture

Thinking and Sharing

After children have worked with two or more bags of blocks, ask volunteers from different groups to share some of their discoveries. Set up a class chart with headings like these to accommodate children's data.

Letter on Bag	Value of Blocks in Bag	Number of Children Sharing	Will there be leftovers?	Number of Units in Each Share	Number of Blocks Left Over

Use prompts like these to promote class discussion:

- When were you able to predict whether you would be able to share the blocks equally with no leftovers? Explain.

- Which bags of blocks could be shared the greatest number of ways with no leftovers? Why do you think this is so?

- Which bags of blocks could be shared the least number of ways? Why do you think this is so?

- What patterns do you see in your data?

Writing

Have children choose one of the bags that they worked with and explain why they had leftovers after having made two or three equal shares.

Teacher Talk

Where's the Mathematics?

This activity gives children the opportunity to make equal shares of a collection of Base Ten Blocks by first trading, if necessary, making groups of equal value and then identifying any leftovers. This experience is important to building an understanding of the division process and the notion of "remainders." Children communicate their thinking and discuss the process of "sharing equally" as they decide how to regroup each set of blocks.

As children go about sharing the blocks in each bag, they determine that it is possible to share some quantities equally and have no leftovers but that it is impossible to share other quantities equally without having leftovers. Children may realize that after counting some groups of blocks, but before distributing them, they will be able to accurately predict whether or not they will have leftovers depending on the number of equal shares they are about to make. Some children will be able to explain their reasoning for determining whether or not there will be leftovers. They may say, for example, that when they share an odd number of blocks between two of them or among four of them they will always have some leftovers.

Looking for patterns in the completed class chart will help children to make the connection between the corresponding fact families for multiplication and division. Children will notice, for example, that a group of blocks shared by three children yields no leftovers if the numbers involved make up a number fact for 3.

$15 \div 3 = 5$ because $5 \times 3 = 15$
$18 \div 3 = 6$ because $6 \times 3 = 18$
$24 \div 3 = 8$ because $8 \times 3 = 24$
$27 \div 3 = 9$ because $9 \times 3 = 27$
$30 \div 3 = 10$ because $10 \times 3 = 30$
$36 \div 3 = 12$ because $12 \times 3 = 36$

Similar conclusions will be drawn for collections of blocks shared by 4 or 5 children.

Extending the Activity

1. Provide children with bags that contain flats as well as longs and units. Have them make two equal shares of the contents, first predicting whether or not there will be leftovers.

2. Allow children to create bags of blocks for others to work with. After filling a bag with blocks, each child must first record the results of making two, three, and four equal shares with those blocks.

As children analyze the division problem implicit in each sharing experience, they will be developing algebraic thinking. Encourage this by showing children how to write a number sentence for each sharing. This will help them to make the connection between the concrete activity and the written symbols that can be used to record it.

Letter on Bag	Value of Blocks in Bag	Number of Children Sharing	Will there be leftovers?	Number of Units in Each Share	Number of Blocks Left Over	
E	25	2	yes	12	1	$25 \div 2 = 12 \text{ R1}$
E	25	3	yes	8	1	$25 \div 3 = 8 \text{ R1}$
E	25	4	yes	6	1	$25 \div 4 = 6 \text{ R1}$
E	25	5	no	5	0	$25 \div 5 = 5$

You can provide for the various ability levels in your classroom by filling the bags with different numbers of blocks. Including flats in some bags will be appropriately challenging for those children who are ready to work with three-place dividends.

MODELING RECTANGLES

- Shape recognition
- Spatial visualization
- Properties of geometric shapes
- Area

Getting Ready

What You'll Need

Base Ten Blocks, 1 set per pair

Small paper bags—some, labeled Length, should contain slips of paper marked 2, 5, 13, 20, 23, 30, 32, and 34; others, labeled Width, should contain 10 slips of paper marked "1–10," 1 of each bag per pair

Base Ten Block Grid Paper, several sheets per pair, page 96

Overhead Base Ten Blocks (optional)

Overview

Children build rectangles using Base Ten longs and units and determine the value of the blocks used to model the rectangles. In this activity, children have the opportunity to:

- understand the attributes of rectangles
- explore the concept of area

The Activity

Introduce the word dimensions *by explaining that the measurements of parts of a figure, such as length and width, are called the* dimensions *of the figure.*

Introducing

- Display this rectangular configuration of Base Ten longs and units and have children copy it.
- Then push the longs and units together to form the rectangle. Establish that the rectangle is 12 units long and 3 units wide.
- Elicit that the *value* of a rectangle is the total number of units used to model it.
- After children determine that the value of this rectangle is 36, call on volunteers to describe different ways they arrived at this value.

On Their Own

> ### How can you use Base 10 Blocks to build a rectangle and find its value?
>
> - Work with a partner. Get a bag that says "Length" and a bag that says "Width."
> - Find the dimensions of a rectangle. Here's how:
>   - Pick 1 slip of paper from the Length bag.
>   - Pick 1 slip of paper from the Width bag.
> - Use blocks to model a rectangle that has the measurements you picked.
> - Record your rectangle on grid paper. (In order to record some rectangles, you will need to tape 2 sheets of grid paper together.)
> - Figure out the value of your rectangle. Record your work.
> - Now, pick again to find the dimensions of another rectangle. Model it with blocks, record it, and find its value. Do this several times.
> - Look for patterns in the sizes of your rectangles and in their values.

The Bigger Picture

Thinking and Sharing

Have children share their results after they have built several rectangles and have found their values. You may wish to have pairs record the dimensions of their rectangles along with the value of each in a chart such as the following. Then record some of these data in a class chart.

RECTANGLES		
Length	Width	Value

Use prompts like these to promote class discussion:

- How did you decide on the number of longs and units to use to build a rectangle?
- How did you go about finding the value of a rectangle?
- How many different rectangles did you build?
- What patterns do you see in your work?
- How could you use the dimensions of the rectangle to find the value of the rectangle?

Writing

Have children model a rectangle with dimensions of their own choosing. Then have them record their rectangle and describe a way to find the value of the rectangle.

Extending the Activity

Alter the numbers on the slips of paper in the "Width" bags so that each indicates a two-digit number. (That is, change the numbers 1 through 10 to

Where's the Mathematics?

Children will go about modeling their rectangles in different ways. You may find that a few pairs will begin by building just the outlines of their rectangles. If you notice this, point out that children should use more blocks to fill in the entire region that their rectangle covers. At first, some pairs may decide to model their rectangles with units alone. They will soon recognize that the more efficient way of modeling is with a combination of longs and units.

Be sure to notice the various ways in which children approach the task of finding the value of their rectangles. Some pairs—even those that used both longs and units to build—may figure out the total value of their rectangle by counting by ones alone. Other pairs may find the number of units in one row of their rectangle and then use repeated addition to find the total value. For example, consider the model one pair built for a 13-by-4 rectangle:

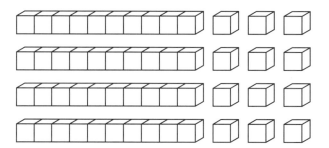

The children determined that one row of their rectangle, made up of 1 long and 3 units, had a value of 13. Since there were four rows of 13, the pair added 13 + 13 + 13 + 13 to find the total value of their rectangle, 52. For the same model, another pair found the value of their longs and the value of their units and then added those sums to find the total value of the rectangle this way: 10 + 10 + 10 + 10 = 40, 3 + 3 + 3 + 3 = 12, and 40 + 12 = 52.

read 11 through 20.) Have children do the activity again, picking slips from these bags, so that they build rectangles with greater dimensions.

This last method will help some children to recognize that the rectangular arrays that they model can also serve as multiplication models. You may want to introduce the multiplication algorithm as a way to record the numbers that the model represents. So, for this model:

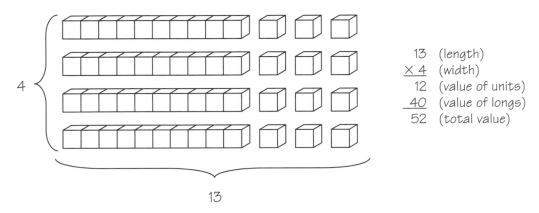

$$
\begin{array}{rl}
13 & \text{(length)} \\
\times\ 4 & \text{(width)} \\
\hline
12 & \text{(value of units)} \\
40 & \text{(value of longs)} \\
\hline
52 & \text{(total value)}
\end{array}
$$

By examining the entries that they have made in the class chart, children will generalize about the patterns they see. These generalizations can set the stage for understanding the formula for finding the area of a rectangle. Some children may notice that the product of multiplying the dimensions of a rectangle is the same as the value of the rectangle. You may then want to explain that the value of a figure is the same as its "area," the number of square units needed to completely cover it.

For those children who seem to be ready to go on, you may want to further explain that there is a formula for finding the area of any rectangle. Point out that a formula is made up of letters that stand for words. Tell children that the formula for the area of a rectangle is *area equals length times width*. Write $A = l \times w$ on the chalkboard and demonstrate how to substitute the dimensions of a rectangle for the letters in the formula to find its area. Challenge pairs to use the formula to record the dimensions and area of one of their rectangles.

NIMBLE NUMBERS

Getting Ready

What You'll Need

Base Ten Blocks, 1 set of longs and units per pair

Overhead Base Ten Blocks (optional)

Overview

In this game for two players, children take turns adding longs and units to a pile in an effort to be the one who puts down the block that brings the value of the pile to 100. In this activity, children have the opportunity to:

◆ count on by tens and ones

◆ use logical reasoning

◆ build mental math skills

◆ develop strategic thinking skills

The Activity

Introducing

◆ Tell children that they are going to play a game called *NIMble Numbers.*

◆ Go over the game rules given in *On Their Own.*

◆ Ask for a volunteer to demonstrate the game with you.

◆ Play a model game, working to reach a target number of 40.

◆ Tell children that they will now play this game using the target number 100.

On Their Own

Play NIMble Numbers!

Here are the rules.

1. This is a game for 2 players. The object is to put down the block that brings the value of the pile of blocks to 100. Players decide who will go first.

2. The first player starts a pile by putting down:

   1 or 2 units
   or
   1 or 2 longs
   or
   1 unit and 1 long.

3. The second player puts down 1 or 2 more blocks and then announces the total value of the blocks in the pile.

4. Players take turns putting down any 1 or 2 blocks and saying each new total. After every turn, the player checks the pile and makes trades from the set, if necessary, to keep the number of blocks in the pile as small as possible.

5. Whoever reaches 100 exactly on a turn is the winner.

- Play the game several times. Take turns going first.
- Look for a winning strategy.

The Bigger Picture

Thinking and Sharing

Invite children to talk about their games and describe some of the thinking they did.

Use prompts like these to promote class discussion:

- ◆ Did winning have anything to do with going first? Explain.
- ◆ How did you decide which blocks and how many of each to play?
- ◆ Did you make any moves that you wanted to take back? Explain.
- ◆ Was there a turning point in the game? If so, what caused it?
- ◆ Did you find a winning strategy? Did it always work?

Writing

1. Have children play the game again, recording the blocks they put down on each turn. When the game is over, have children look back at the blocks they played and tell what they might do differently if they could replay a turn.

2. Have children describe a strategy for winning at *NIMble Numbers*. Their strategy may be one that they developed for themselves or one that they learned during class discussion.

Teacher Talk

Where's the Mathematics?

The name of this activity, *NIMble Numbers,* reflects its connection to the ancient Chinese game NIM, for which there is a strategy for winning. Most children will begin to play this game without a strategy in mind, randomly choosing combinations of blocks to contribute to the pile. After playing the game several times, however, children may come to realize that there are important numbers to reach along the way. Once having reached one of those numbers, a thoughtful player should be able to win the game.

Children will notice that there are five possible block values that they can contribute to the pile on a turn:

Number of Blocks	Blocks Used	Block Values
1	1 unit	1
1	1 long	10
2	1 unit and 1 long	11
2	2 units	2
2	2 longs	20

As they discuss and analyze the game as it progresses, children communicate their mathematical thinking and solidify their reasoning. They may think that they have identified a good strategy for winning because it seemed to have worked once. Point out that is necessary to play the game several times to see whether or not a strategy works every time.

Extending the Activity

Ask children to suggest some ideas for making up a new strategy game by changing a few of the rules for *NIMble Numbers.*

Some children may realize that one way of gaining control of the game is by making sure that strategic values are reached along the way. They may note that there is a winning follow-up play for each strategic value. (And, they must try to keep their opponents from being able to make these plays.) A few children will understand why these values are strategic. Others may have a notion of why but be unable to explain it.

A player will be able to win on one play if it is his or her turn to put down blocks when the pile has one of the following strategic values. The strategic values given are listed working backward from the target number, 100:

Strategic Values	Winning Plays	This Works Because:
99	1 unit	99 + 1 = 100
98	2 units	98 + 2 = 100
90	1 long	90 + 10 = 100
89	1 long and 1 unit	89 + 11 = 100
80	2 longs	80 + 20 = 100

Children may extend this list, finding other strategic values by continuing backward from 80.

1,000, MORE OR LESS

- Addition
- Place value
- Estimation
- Mental math

Getting Ready

What You'll Need

Base Ten Blocks, 1 set per group

Base Ten Blocks Place-Value Mat (optional), 1 per pair

Number cubes marked 1 to 6, 3 per group

Overhead Base Ten Blocks (optional)

Overview

Children model a 3-digit starting number with Base Ten Blocks. They roll number cubes to help them determine another 3-digit number that, when added to the starting number, will result in a sum that is close to 1,000. In this activity, children have the opportunity to:

- ◆ find missing addends
- ◆ develop strategies for adding 3-digit numbers
- ◆ use logical reasoning
- ◆ build mental math skills

The Activity

You can further evaluate children's understanding of place value if you have them work with a 3-digit house number that has a zero in either the tens or ones place. Look for children's responses to being asked to suggest other 3-digit numbers that can be made from the digits in this kind of number.

Introducing

- ◆ Call on volunteers to name their house numbers. Write the numbers on the board as children say them.
- ◆ Continue asking for house numbers until you have recorded at least one 3-digit number.
- ◆ Circle a 3-digit house number and ask children to model it with Base Ten Blocks.
- ◆ Ask volunteers to identify other 3-digit numbers that can be formed from the same 3 digits in the number you circled. Record these numbers on the board and have children model them.

On Their Own

What 3-digit number can you add to a starting number modeled with Base 10 Blocks to get a sum that is close to 1,000?

- Work with a partner. Make up a 3-digit number between 300 and 700. This is your starting number.

- Record your starting number. Then use Base 10 Blocks to model it. Keep this model.

- Roll 3 number cubes and record the digits that come up.

- What 3-digit numbers can you make from the digits you rolled? Record them.

- Decide which of the 3-digit numbers to add to your starting number to get a sum close to 1,000.

- Try it! First use blocks to model the 3-digit number of your choice. Then put these blocks together with the blocks that model your starting number. Trade, if necessary. What is the sum of all the blocks?

- Is the sum close to 1,000? Could you have gotten closer if you had added a number made up of a different arrangement of your 3 digits? If you think you could, try it. Record your findings.

- Now make up a different starting number. Roll the 3 number cubes again and repeat the activity.

- Be ready to share your strategies for getting a sum close to 1,000.

The Bigger Picture

Thinking and Sharing

Once each pair has done the activity twice, have children discuss which sets of sums were closest to 1,000. Call children together to discuss what they noticed.

Use prompts like these to promote class discussion:

- How did you decide on a starting number?

- What is the least possible sum of your starting number and one of the 3-digit numbers you rolled? What is the greatest possible sum?

- With what kind of starting numbers could you be sure to get a sum that is less than 1,000?

- After rolling the number cubes, how did you decide on which 3-digit number to add to your starting number?

- How could you prove that the number you added to your starting number was the one that brought the sum closest to 1,000?

- If you did the activity again, what would you choose as a starting number? Explain.

Extending the Activity

Have two to four children use this activity as a game. Each child selects a starting number between 300 and 700, records it, and models it with blocks. Someone rolls the three number cubes. Players all list the possible 3-digit numbers for the digits that come up. Children decide which of the 3-digit

Teacher Talk

Where's the Mathematics?

By estimating sums as called for in *1,000, More or Less,* children strengthen their number and operational senses. They may approach this activity in a variety of ways. Some children will begin by randomly selecting a starting number. Others will begin by considering all the possible outcomes of rolling three number cubes and then use this data as a determinant in making up a starting number. These children will notice that the highest roll possible, 666, results from rolling all sixes and that the lowest roll possible, 111, results from rolling all ones. Based on this, they may see why the activity gives 300 as the minimum starting number. Children who realize how unlikely it is to roll either 3 sixes or 3 ones will come to see why the activity tells them to choose a starting number that falls somewhere between 300 and 700. Most children will reach this understanding only after completing the activity several times.

In order to determine which 3-digit number is the best to model, some children will round the starting number and each of the 3-digit numbers to the hundreds place, model each with flats, and then estimate the sum by counting each group of flats. Other children will round each number to the nearest ten, using flats and longs to come up with even closer estimates. Estimating in this way builds on children's understanding of place value. The chart that follows shows the work of one pair of children that rounded to estimate the sum of their starting number and each of the possible 3-digit numbers. They chose a starting number of 520; rolled the digits 1, 4, and 6; and then estimated by rounding to the nearest ten:

60 THE SUPER SOURCE® ◆ Base Ten Blocks ◆ Grades 3–4   © ETA/Cuisenaire®

numbers to model based on their starting numbers. Players each combine the blocks for the number of their choice with the blocks for their own starting number. Together children determine how close each sum is to 1,000. The *difference* between a player's sum and 1,000 becomes his or her score for the round. After playing several rounds, whoever has the *lowest* total score wins.

Starting Number ⟶ 520

Digits Rolled ⟶ 1, 4, 6

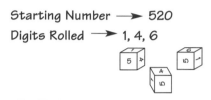

3-Digit Number	Estimated Sum
146	520 + 150 = 670
164	520 + 160 = 680
416	520 + 420 = 940
461	520 + 460 = 980
614	520 + 610 = 1,130
641	520 + 640 = 1,160

By charting and reviewing their data in this way, the pair could easily see that 461 would be the best choice of 3-digit numbers, as adding it to 520 would bring them closest to 1,000.

Children will find some shortcuts as they work. Even before they roll the number cubes they may subtract their starting number from 1,000 to get an idea of the magnitude of the digits they would need to roll. Using Base Ten Blocks to model this kind of subtraction is easier and more satisfying for children than paper-and-pencil subtraction would be.

Although most children will not begin the activity with a strategy in mind, trial and error will lead them to notice whether or not their choice of 3-digit numbers brought them as close to 1,000 as possible. After they have done the activity at least twice, children should be encouraged to stop and assess what seems to work and what does not. They will learn from one another as they discuss and share their thinking. The most important lesson that children learn from this activity is that there are many different—legitimate—ways to solve a problem.

PLACE IT

- Addition
- Estimation
- Place value
- Game strategies

Getting Ready

What You'll Need

Base Ten Blocks, 1 set per group

Put-in-Place Mats, 1 per child, page 90

Number cube marked 1 to 6, 2 per group

Overhead Base Ten Blocks and/or Put-in-Place Mat transparency (optional)

Overview

In this game for two to four players, children each roll number cubes and then make a 2-digit number from the digits rolled. They represent that number with units and longs in an effort to be the one who accumulates blocks with the total value closest to 100. In this activity, children have the opportunity to:

- ◆ do mental computation
- ◆ develop strategic thinking skills

The Activity

Be sure that children understand the conditions for scoring a rejected throw. Point out that once blocks are placed on a turn they may not be changed or rejected.

Introducing

- ◆ Tell children that you rolled a pair of number cubes and that "...these two digits came up." Write 6 on the chalkboard. Then write 2 below the 6.
- ◆ Ask a volunteer to come to the board and rewrite these digits as a 2-digit number. Have another volunteer write the same digits as a different 2-digit number.
- ◆ Invite several pairs of children to roll two number cubes and then name two different 2-digit numbers for each roll.
- ◆ Explain the game rules given in *On Their Own*.
- ◆ Demonstrate by playing a partial game of *Place It* with a volunteer.

On Their Own

Play *Place It!*

Here are the rules.

1. This is a game for 2 to 4 players. The object is to get blocks that have a total value close to 100 without going over.

2. A player rolls the number cubes and decides how to read the digits that come up as a 2-digit number. The player takes units and longs to show that number and places the blocks on a mat that looks like this.

PUT-IN-PLACE MAT

Round	LONGS	UNITS
1		

3. The other players each take a turn rolling the number cubes, deciding on 2-digit numbers, and placing blocks on their mats to show their numbers.

4. Play continues for a total of 5 rounds.

5. A player may reject any 1 throw if it seems that either of the 2-digit numbers would add too much to his or her sum. Each player may do this *only once* during a game. The player must count a rejected throw as 1 of the 5 rounds by giving it a score of 0 for the round.

6. After 5 rounds, players find the total values of their blocks and record them. Whoever gets closest to 100 without going over is the winner.

- Play 4 games of *Place It!*
- Be ready to talk about good moves and bad moves.

The Bigger Picture

Thinking and Sharing

Invite children to talk about their games and describe some of the thinking they did.

Use prompts like these to promote class discussion:

- ◆ How did you decide which 2-digit number to use on each roll?
- ◆ Were you ever sorry that you didn't use the other number you rolled? Explain.
- ◆ Did you ever decide to reject a throw? If so, tell why.
- ◆ How did you decide whose sum was closest to 100?
- ◆ Do you have a strategy for winning this game? Do you think that it will always work? Tell about it.

Writing

Have children record the numbers that they used for one game. Suggest that they look at this data and describe how they might have changed one number or another in order to get closer to 100.

Teacher Talk

Where's the Mathematics?

As children first consider the reasonableness of modeling one number or the other on each turn and also consider whether or not to reject the digits rolled altogether, they are exercising their critical-thinking ability. Keeping either an estimated sum or an actual running sum of the value of the two-digit numbers they model strengthens their number and operational senses.

Children may devise a variety of strategies for reaching 100 as they play this game. Some may always choose the lesser 2-digit number in each of the first few rounds as a buffer against rolling pairs of high digits in later rounds. Others may aim to get as close to 100 as possible on the first four rolls knowing they can use the reject option on their last roll.

In the first game shown below, Player A chose to model the lesser number possible for each of the first four rounds and then to reject the throw for the fifth round. This strategy proved to be successful. It is likely that as the game progressed, Player B regretted not having modeled the lesser number in round two. If so, that player probably learned that when faced with a high digit and a low one in the early rounds of a game, it generally makes sense to model the lesser number.

Player A

PUT-IN-PLACE MAT		
Round	LONGS	UNITS
1	I	..
2	II	......
3	II	......
4	III	.....
5	Reject	Throw
TOTAL ➝ 99 (WINS)		

Digits Rolled

2 and 1

2 and 6

2 and 6

5 and 3

3 and 1

Player B

PUT-IN-PLACE MAT		
Round	LONGS	UNITS
1	II	.
2	IIIIII	..
3	II	......
4	Reject	Throw
5	I	...
TOTAL ⟶ 122		

The more games children play the more some of them may come to decide that strategy might not matter after all. They may begin to realize that chance plays an important part in this game because, on each roll, there are equally likely chances of rolling any combination of the digits 1 to 6. Therefore, implementing what would seem to be a winning strategy will not always result in a win. Players C and D learned this when their game ended with no winner because both totals went above 100.

Extending the Activity

1. Have children play another game of *Place It,* this time playing so that the winner is the one whose total is closest to 100 even if it goes *above* 100.

2. Children can play by rolling *three* number cubes and using the digits rolled to make 3-digit numbers. (Adjust the *Put-in-Place* mat for this game by inserting a column labeled "Flats" to the left of the "Longs" column.) The children agree on a target number between 700 and 1,000. The winner is the one who gets closest to that number without going over it.

Player C

Round	LONGS	UNITS
1	IIII	......
2	III	.....
3	I	.....
4	II	...
5	Reject	Throw
TOTAL	⟶	119

PUT-IN-PLACE MAT

Digits Rolled

4 and 6

5 and 3

1 and 5

3 and 2

6 and 6

Player D

PUT-IN-PLACE MAT

Round	LONGS	UNITS
1	Reject	Throw
2	III	.....
3	I	.....
4	II	...
5	IIIIII	......
TOTAL	⟶	139

Rolling high digits can prove less frustrating when playing the version of the game in which the winner is the one who gets the total closest to 100 even if that total goes *above* 100. Players E and F rolled only high digits throughout their game, so even using the lesser of the two possible numbers for each round produced totals that were both well above 100. In this case, Player F was the winner with a total of 171.

Player E

PUT-IN-PLACE MAT

Round	LONGS	UNITS
1	IIIII	......
2	Reject	Throw
3	III	.....
4	IIIII	.....
5	IIII	......
TOTAL	⟶	192

Digits Rolled

5 and 6

4 and 3

5 and 3

5 and 5

6 and 4

Player F

PUT-IN-PLACE MAT

Round	LONGS	UNITS
1	IIIII	......
2	III	....
3	III	......
4	Reject	Throw
5	IIII	......
TOTAL	⟶	171 (WINS)

Children will have different ways of keeping their running totals. Some may need to recount their blocks before each roll. Others may estimate their totals by tallying the longs only, forgetting about the units altogether—later to find that the units bring their total over 100. Children should become aware of the possible need to trade at the end of a round.

As children play they communicate strategies and discuss choices. This helps them to solidify and deepen their understanding of place value, numerical relationships, and the algorithm for regrouping in addition.

RIDDLE ME THIS

Getting Ready

What You'll Need

Base Ten Blocks, 1 set per pair

3" × 5" cards, several per pair

paper bags, 1 per pair

paper clips, 1 per pair

Overhead Base Ten Blocks (optional)

Overview

Children model a number using Base Ten Blocks and then hide their model. They create clues to help others guess what number they modeled and which blocks they used to model it. In this activity, children have the opportunity to:

◆ use place-value terminology

◆ communicate about mathematical concepts

◆ use logical reasoning

The Activity

Introducing

◆ Prepare a "riddle bag" by putting 1 flat, 3 longs, and 2 units into a paper bag and closing it.

◆ Display the closed bag and tell children that you will give them a set of clues to help them answer the riddle "Which blocks are in this bag and what number do they model?"

◆ Write the following clues on the board.

There are 6 blocks in the bag.
They model a number that is greater than 100 and less than 200.
There are exactly 3 longs.
Which blocks are in this bag and what number do they model?

◆ Have children use blocks to model the solution.

◆ When they are ready, have children display their solutions. Then reveal the contents of the riddle bag so they can check their work.

◆ Ask children to tell how they used each clue to help them solve.

◆ Discuss what constitutes a good clue. Then point out that a good set of clues leads to just one solution.

On Their Own

How would you write a set of clues about Base 10 Blocks for a number riddle?

- Work with a partner. Use Base 10 Blocks to show any 2-digit or 3-digit number.

- Examine your blocks and take turns describing the number to each other in different ways.

- Talk about clues that you could give about your blocks to help others answer the riddle *"Which blocks are in this bag and what number do they model?"*

- Write down your best clues on a card.

- Now test your clues. Are you sure that others could use them to solve the riddle? Do you need to change any clues? Do you need to add any?

- When you are satisfied with your clues, do this.
  - Put your blocks into a bag.
  - Close the bag.
  - Clip the card to the bag.

- Exchange riddle bags with another pair. Follow the other pair's clues to solve the riddle. Use blocks to model the solution. Then look into the bag to check your answer.

The Bigger Picture

Thinking and Sharing

Invite children to talk about how they wrote and tested their own clues and how they followed the other pair's clues.

Use prompts like these to promote class discussion:

- How did you decide what clues to use?

- What words did you use to describe your number?

- Was it easier to write clues or to follow them? Why?

- After reading one of the other pair's clues, were you ever sure that certain blocks were *not* in the bag? Explain.

- Does the order of the clues in a set matter?

- Did you have to use all the clues to solve the riddle?

- Did any set of clues lead to more than one solution? If so, how could you change some of the clues so that there would be just one solution?

Have children use Base Ten Blocks to show one number in two different ways. Tell them that, for example, they can represent the number 21 either

Teacher Talk

Where's the Mathematics?

If children have difficulty following the riddle clues in the *Introducing* activity, have them work with a place-value mat. Point out that the first clue tells them that they will need to put a total of 6 blocks on their mat. Elicit that the second clue suggests that they will need 1 flat (to represent a number greater than 100, but less than 200). The third clue, probably the easiest for children to interpret, tells them that they should put 3 longs on their mat. Now, having 4 blocks, and remembering that they need a total of 6, children should realize that they need to add 2 units to their mat. These 6 blocks model the number 132.

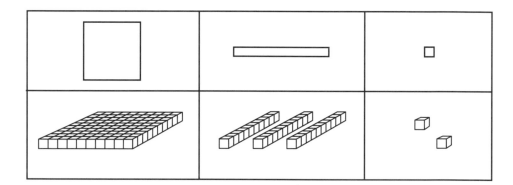

Children will probably find that it is easier to follow clues than to write them. Even though they may feel a certain comfort level in using their own words to communicate their ideas, they will find that trying to write a meaningful clue can be difficult. The task of writing clues helps children become aware of the importance of using precise mathematical language.

Clues that identify the total number of blocks and those that suggest the number of each kind of block are probably the easiest to write. Children will have more difficulty writing clues that suggest place value and those that indicate the specific value of the number. Initially, children's clues will need to be checked for accuracy. Look for imprecise wording. Be alert for clues that "give away" either the number itself or the number of each kind of hidden block. Finally, be sure that there are enough clues in a set so that it is possible for other children to use them to identify the hidden blocks and the number they represent.

with 2 longs and 1 unit or with 1 long and 11 units. Once they have decided on the two ways to model their number, have children write a set of clues for each way of modeling it.

As they begin to write, children may group clues into categories. They may find it worthwhile to begin with general clues, such as, "There are 4 blocks," and then go on to write more specific clues, such as, "There are 2 more longs than units." The following sets of clues were written by two pairs of children for the blocks shown below. Notice which set of clues is better and why.

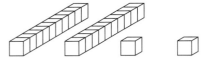

There are 2 longs.	*There are 4 blocks.*
There are no flats.	*The number is less than 100.*
The number is even.	*There is the same number of longs as units.*

Clearly, the set of clues on the left has more than one solution. You may want to present it to children and challenge them to add to or change one or more of the clues to make the set lead to just one solution.

Children will develop their own strategies for using clues to solve the riddle. They may realize that the order in which the clues are presented can affect the difficulty. Some children may first read all the clues and then try to satisfy those that seem either most important, most difficult, or most useful. Other children may follow the clues in order, from first to last, evaluating the possibilities as they work. Children may also use the strategy of mentally combining clues.

The skills of writing and following clues can be improved over time. Consider revisiting this activity periodically throughout the school year to provide children with additional opportunities to build these skills.

SCHOOL SIZES

- Area
- Spatial visualization
- Estimation

Getting Ready

What You'll Need

Base Ten Blocks, 1 set per pair

School Floor Plans, 1 set per pair, pages 91, 92 (cut apart)

Black marker

Base Ten Block Grid paper, 1 sheet per child, page 96

Overhead Base Ten Blocks and/or School Floor Plans transparencies (optional)

Overview

Children estimate the area of irregular polygons. Then they use Base Ten Blocks to determine the actual area of each. In this activity, children have the opportunity to:

- ◆ explore the concept of area
- ◆ use estimation skills
- ◆ use spatial reasoning

The Activity

Introducing

- ◆ Use the marker to write the word "HAT" in capital letters on Base Ten Block Grid Paper.

  (Be sure to darken the grid lines that fall within the letter outlines so that children cannot see them.) Make and distribute copies.

  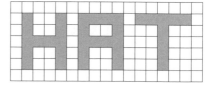

- ◆ Tell children that you want to find out which letter is the biggest. Ask them to estimate the number of unit blocks that they would need to cover each letter exactly. Record several estimates for each letter.

- ◆ Have children cover their letters with unit blocks. Ask the class to tell which letter is the biggest and why.

On Their Own

Which school floor plan is the biggest? Which is the smallest?

- Work with a partner and school floor plans that look like these.

- Which floor plan do you think is the biggest? the smallest? Estimate. Then put the floor plans in order, from biggest to smallest. Record your estimate.

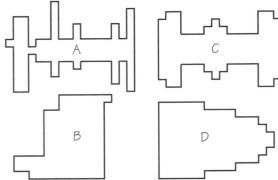

- Use longs and units to find the exact size of any 1 floor plan. Trade blocks when necessary. Record the exact size.

- Do you want to change your estimate based on your finding? If so, change the way you put the plans in order *now*.

- Find and record the size of each of the other floor plans.

- Now put the plans in order, from biggest to smallest, according to their actual sizes. How good were your estimates?

The Bigger Picture

Thinking and Sharing

Discuss one floor plan at a time and invite children to tell how they estimated its size. Ask pairs to share how they decided which blocks to use to find the actual size. As children discuss their results, make a two-column list for each floor plan, recording children's estimates for the plan in one column and the actual size of the plan in the other.

Use prompts like these to promote class discussion:

- ◆ On what did you base your estimate?
- ◆ What method did you use for comparing the floor plans?
- ◆ Did you find any shortcuts for using the blocks? Explain.
- ◆ How close was your estimate of the order to the actual order?
- ◆ Did you ever think that you could tell the actual size of a plan without measuring it? How could you tell?

Writing

Have children choose one of the school floor plans and designate regions of it for specific uses. Then have them describe why they think those regions would be good for the uses they cited.

Extending the Activity

1. Establish that the *area* of a region is the amount of surface the region covers. Area is measured in square units. The area of one face of a Base Ten unit block measures 1 square centimeter (1 cm^2).

   Have children create their own school floor plan by first arranging Base Ten Blocks on grid paper to form a "school" and then holding the blocks in place on the grid paper as they trace around them. Each child should

Teacher Talk

Where's the Mathematics?

This activity gives children an opportunity to build an intuitive understanding of area and to develop strategies for finding the area of irregular shapes. Through this hands-on investigation, children begin to understand that area is expressed as the number of square units that cover a region.

Children's estimates will vary based on their previous experience in using Base Ten Blocks and in working with activities that involve spatial relationships. Children estimate the size of the floor plans and then order them. Then they find the actual "size" (area) of one plan. After comparing the actual size with their estimates of the size, children have a chance to refine their estimates and reorder the floor plans. This exercise gives children the chance to evaluate their own estimation strategies. They then apply what they have just discovered and use it to focus on the sizes of the remaining plans. This helps them to make educated estimates rather than guesses.

Children will use Base Ten Blocks in various ways to determine the area of the floor plans. Some children may decide to cover a plan using units alone. They will soon discover that the use of both longs and units makes the

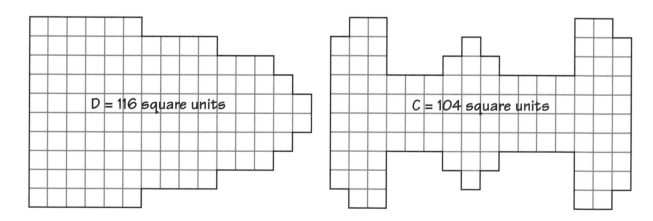

find the area of his or her floor plan and record it on another piece of paper as a number of square centimeters. Then have children exchange grid papers and use blocks to find the area of one another's plans.

2. Designate a target number for the area of a school (or other structure) and have children design a floor plan with that area.

---

process more efficient. Other children will see a floor plan as having separate, distinct sections. They may fill each section with blocks, counting the units they used in each section, and then find the sum of the units in all the sections. Still other children may cover sections with blocks, forming rectangles that extend beyond the plan in some places. After finding the total number of blocks in such a rectangle, they may then subtract a unit for each space that falls outside the plan. Of course, children who choose to first fill a plan with as many longs as possible and then use units to fill in the empty spaces will have found the most efficient approach.

Although there is just one solution to this problem, children will have many different methods for measuring each floor plan with blocks and then comparing the sizes of the plans. Children will benefit from communicating their methods for estimating, counting, and finding area. They will gain an appreciation for the many and varied ways there are for approaching a problem. As children compare and discuss their solutions, they analyze the differences and similarities in their work and use Base Ten Blocks to check their accuracy in counting and measuring.

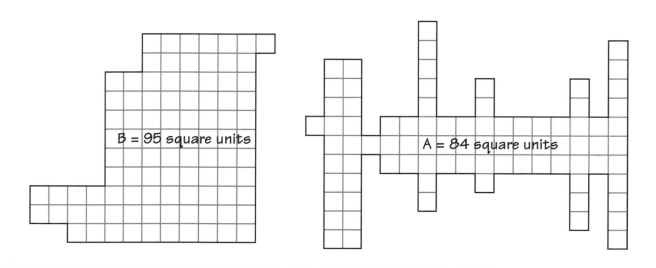

B = 95 square units

A = 84 square units

TEN, TEN, TEN

Getting Ready

What You'll Need

Base Ten Blocks, 1 set per group

Base Ten Blocks Place-Value Mat, 1 per child

Number cubes marked 1 to 6, 2 per group

Number cubes marked 4 to 9, 1 per group (For an easier game, have children use 1-to-6 number cubes only, 3 per group.)

Ten, Ten, Ten Score Sheet, 1 per child, page 93

Overhead Base Ten Blocks (optional)

Overview

In this game for two to four players, children take turns rolling three number cubes and finding the sum of the numbers they roll in an effort to be the one with the highest score at the end of the game. In this activity, children have the opportunity to:

- ◆ apply strategies for adding 1-digit numbers
- ◆ look for addition combinations to 10
- ◆ develop strategic thinking skills

The Activity

Introducing

- ◆ Display the three number cubes that you want children to use for the game *Ten, Ten, Ten*. Tell children that you rolled these three cubes and that the digits 4, 1, and 6 came up. Write these digits on the chalkboard.

- ◆ Direct children to take enough unit blocks to model each digit and then put all of these units on a place-value mat.

- ◆ Now tell children to find the sum of the units, either by adding the numbers or by counting the units and trading for a long, if necessary.

- ◆ Ask if any two of the digits rolled have a sum of exactly 10.

- ◆ Elicit that 4 and 6 have a sum of 10.

- ◆ Explain that because two of the digits add up to 10, each of the children may take a bonus block with a value of 10 (1 long) and put it on his or her mat.

- ◆ Establish that children will play a game in which they will keep their own scores. (Point out that your score in this round of the game would be 21 because the sum of 4, 1, and 6 is 11, and 11 plus 10 bonus points equals 21.)

- ◆ Go over the game rules given in *On Their Own*.

On Their Own

Play Ten, Ten, Ten!

Here are the rules.

1. This is a game for 2 to 4 players. The object is to get the highest score. Players decide who will go first.

2. A player rolls 3 number cubes. Then that player
   - takes Base 10 unit blocks to model each digit rolled,
   - puts the units on a place-value mat, and
   - trades 10 units for 1 long, if possible.

3. Players each keep a score sheet that looks like this.

═══ TEN, TEN, TEN SCORE SHEET ═══

Round	Digits Rolled	Sum of Digits	10 Bonus Points (if 2 digits equal 10)	Score for Round

4. Whoever rolls 2 digits with a sum of exactly 10 gets 10 bonus points! (This means putting 1 more long on the mat and adding 10 extra points to the score.)

5. Players take turns rolling the number cubes, putting blocks on their mats, and finding their scores.

6. After 10 rounds, players find the total value of their blocks. They record their total. Whoever has the highest score wins the game.

- Play 2 games of Ten, Ten, Ten!
- Be ready to talk about your games.

The Bigger Picture

Thinking and Sharing

Invite children to talk about their games and describe some of the thinking they did.

Use prompts like these to promote class discussion:

- What did you notice about playing this game?
- Did the player who got the most 10-point bonuses always win?
- How many different ways could you roll a sum of 10 with two number cubes?
- Did you ever roll 3 fives? If so, how many bonus points did you get for the roll?
- What are some of your scores? Are most of them close together or far apart? Explain.

Extending the Activity

Have children play the game again using *three* 4-to-9 number cubes. In this game, a player gets the 10-point bonus for rolling a sum of 15 on two of the three cubes.

Teacher Talk

Where's the Mathematics?

Ten, Ten, Ten, unlike the other games in this book, is a game of chance, not of strategy. Children's scores, therefore, will depend on the random rolls of three number cubes. But it is only when they are alert to opportunities for picking up bonus points that children will attain their greatest potential scores.

Even when presented with just three single-digit numbers, many children fail to identify sums of 10 at a glance. By providing children with the motivation to instantly sight the basic facts of 10, this activity helps to strengthen their understanding of the workings of our Base Ten number system, crucial to their later work with greater numbers.

After rolling the number cubes, some children may need to count, one unit at a time, for each digit rolled and then recount all the units to find the sum of the digits. Other children will find the sum of two of the three digits mentally and then count on to include the third digit in the sum. These children will see how finding a sum of 10 speeds up the addition process. (They may say that it's easy to mentally add one more digit to 10.) After playing a few rounds of their first game, children will begin to notice combinations of 10 more quickly than they did at first, keeping in mind that each 10 will get them a bonus.

Rolling 3 fives at once raises the question of whether the player is entitled to 10 bonus points or to 20! A game rule states: *Whoever rolls 2 digits with a sum of exactly 10 gets 10 bonus points!* Children who have rolled 3 fives are likely to be quick to claim that because there are two different ways to get a sum of exactly 10, they should be entitled to two sets of bonus points, or 20 points. Address this issue even if no one has rolled 3 fives as yet. (It's likely to happen soon!) Lead children to decide how they will score this situation if it occurs.

You may want to interrupt the play after several rounds in order to have children determine all the possible ways they could get a sum of 10 on two of the three cubes. You can help them compile their findings by setting up a chart like the one below. Children will see that they can get sums of 10 by rolling any combination of 5 and 5 or 4 and 6 on any two of the three cubes.

**Ways to Roll Sums
of 10 on Two of Three
1-to-6 Number Cubes:**

4	6	–
5	5	–
6	4	–
6	–	4
4	–	6
–	4	6
–	5	5
–	6	4

If children roll two 1-to-6 cubes and one 4-to-9 cube, then they can get sums of 10 by rolling any combination of 5 and 5, 4 and 6, 7 and 3, 8 and 2, and 9 and 1. Eventually, some children may say that since there are more fours and sixes than any other number on these three cubes, combinations of 4 and 6 are likely to be rolled more often than other combinations.

WHADDA CARD!

Getting Ready

What You'll Need

Base Ten Blocks, up to 81 cubes and 90 longs per pair*

Whadda Card! Spinner, page 94
1 per pair

Base Ten Block Grid Paper, several sheets per pair

Packs of 3" × 5" index cards, from 1 to 9 cards per pack, 1 pack per pair

Overhead Base Ten Blocks (optional)

Overview

Children create addition and/or multiplication models by placing equal numbers of Base Ten Blocks of a kind on index cards according to the spin of a spinner. They then record the number sentences that their models represent. In this activity, children have the opportunity to:

- practice addition
- recognize that multiplication is a process of repeated addition
- use patterns to predict products

The Activity

The number of units and longs that children will need depends on the number of cards in the pack they take. If the numbers of Base Ten Blocks indicated above are not available, then reduce the maximum number of cards in a pack from nine to six.

Introducing

- Ask two volunteers to hold out their hands, palms up.
- Count out 2 units into each hand. Ask children how they can find the number of units in the four hands.
- Lead children to count the units by twos. Write this on the chalkboard as the addition sentence $2 + 2 + 2 + 2 = 8$.
- Elicit that 2 units in each of 4 hands means that there is a total of 8 units. Point out that because the same number, 2, is added 4 times, another way of recording this is with multiplication.
- Write the multiplication sentence $4 \times 2 = 8$ on the board. Read it aloud as "Four twos equal eight."
- Ask children to suggest ways to record 2 cubes in each of 4 hands on grid paper.

On Their Own

How many different ways can you cover each card from a pack with equal numbers of Base 10 Blocks?

- Work with a partner. Take a pack of index cards.

- How many cards are in your pack? Spread out the cards. Then spin a spinner that looks like this.

- What did you spin? Put that number of unit blocks on each card.

- Think: *How many cards? How many units on each?* Find the value of the units. Record your work on grid paper.

- Now clear off the units. Put an equal number of longs in their place.

- Now think: *How many cards? How many longs on each?* Find the value of the longs. Record your work on grid paper.

- Compare the values you found for the units and for the same number of longs. What do you notice?

- Repeat the activity several times. (If you spin the same number as before, just spin again!)

- Be ready to talk about what you did and what you found out.

The Bigger Picture

Thinking and Sharing

Write the numbers 1 through 9 across the board. Have volunteers, one pair at a time, post their recordings under the number that matches their number of cards. Review children's work, column by column, having each pair tell what they recorded for each number of units and longs that they spun.

Use prompts like these to promote class discussion:

- What do you notice about the posted work?

- What was the least number of units that you could get on any turn? What was the greatest number of units?

- What was the least number of longs that you could get on any turn? What was the greatest number of longs?

- Are all the number facts posted for addition? for multiplication? Which fact(s) are missing in each column?

- How is what you recorded for a number of units like what you recorded for the same number of longs? How is it different?

Writing

Have children explain how to find the total number of student chairs in a classroom that has five rows with eight chairs in each row.

Teacher Talk

Where's the Mathematics?

This activity may be used either to introduce the concept of multiplication or to reinforce what children already know. Children connect what they model with the concrete manipulatives to what they record with abstract symbols as they write number sentences for the units and longs that they position for each spin. How children record their numbers of blocks will depend upon their understanding of addition and multiplication.

You will probably need to assemble multiple sets of index cards in order to have enough sets for each pair. Make sure that at least one pack of each size is being used by at least one pair of children so that every factor from 1 through 9 will be covered.

Once children begin spinning the spinner and placing blocks on their cards they will realize that the number of cards in a pack represents their one (constant) factor. Children who pick the smallest pack (1 card) will be modeling facts of 1. Those who pick the next larger pack (2 cards) will model facts of 2, and so on. Some children may use words to record what they model; for example, "3 groups of 2 is 6." Others may record their models as repeated addition and/or as multiplication; for example, $2 + 2 + 2 = 6$ and/or $3 \times 2 = 6$.

Children will depict their models on grid paper in different ways. Some may fill in arrays of squares, others will outline arrays. You may wish to encourage children to cut out their arrays so that they can post them individually in the class chart.

Because the postings in each column of the class chart are likely to contain both addition and multiplication sentences, you may chose to quickly acknowledge the correct addition sentences and then focus on the multiplication sentences. Call on children to supply any basic multiplication facts that may be missing from particular columns. If you notice that any fact missing from one column appears with its factors reversed in another column, test children's ability to informally recognize the commutative property of multiplication by challenging them to find the fact elsewhere

Extending the Activity

1. Have pairs exchange packs of cards and do the activity again using the new number of cards as their constant factor.

2. Ask children to look back over what they recorded for one of their spins. Challenge them to imagine using flats, in place of units or longs, for this spin. Tell them to think about how they can use what they recorded for units and longs to help them find the total value of equal numbers of flats.

---

on the chart. Then have whoever correctly identifies the fact rewrite it with its factors reversed and post an array for it in the appropriate column.

Draw children's attention to pairs of multiplication sentences that represent the modeling of an equal number of units and longs. To help children readily see the relationships, you may want to rewrite related facts, one above the other. For example, if a pair with four cards spins 7, you would write the following:

$$7 + 7 + 7 + 7 = 28 \qquad\qquad 4 \times 7 = 28$$
$$70 + 70 + 70 + 70 = 280 \qquad 4 \times 70 = 280$$

If you have a large supply of flats available, have pairs use them to extend some of the work they did using units and longs. Call on volunteers to read the number sentences that they model with flats. Align these below the related number sentences as, for the example above:

$$7 + 7 + 7 + 7 = 28 \qquad\qquad 4 \times 7 = 28$$
$$70 + 70 + 70 + 70 = 280 \qquad 4 \times 70 = 280$$
$$\mathbf{700 + 700 + 700 + 700 = 2{,}800} \qquad \mathbf{4 \times 700 = 2{,}800}$$

Lead children to look for number patterns in the related facts. (They will probably notice the pattern of the increasing numbers of zeros.) You may then want to ask children what number sentences they could write if they could replace the flats on the cards with thousands cubes. For the example above, they could write:

$$\mathbf{7{,}000 + 7{,}000 + 7{,}000 + 7{,}000 = 28{,}000} \qquad \mathbf{4 \times 7{,}000 = 28{,}000}$$

This activity helps children understand the concept of multiplication as they develop visual images for multiplication facts. You may want to leave this activity available at a math center so that children can gain further practice with other factor pairs each time they do the activity using different numbers of cards.

WHAT AMOUNTS?

Getting Ready

What You'll Need

Base Ten Blocks, 1 set per pair

Overhead Base Ten Blocks (optional)

Overview

Children look for ways to use a combination of four Base Ten Blocks to model as many different numbers as possible. In this activity, children have the opportunity to:

- ◆ develop understanding of place value
- ◆ build number sense
- ◆ organize information
- ◆ look for patterns

The Activity

Introducing

- ◆ Have each child take two flats, two longs, and two units.
- ◆ Ask children to choose any two of these blocks and put them together to model a number.
- ◆ Call on a volunteer to suggest one combination of blocks and the number it represents. Record the amount on the chalkboard.
- ◆ Have volunteers suggest other numbers that they can model with just two of the six blocks.
- ◆ Record and discuss each of the possible solutions.

On Their Own

How many different numbers can you model with 4 Base 10 Blocks?

- With a partner take any combination of 4 Base 10 Blocks. Choose from flats, longs, and units.

- Use all of your blocks to model any amount.

- Decide on a way to record the number of each kind of block and the amount you modeled.

- Now take a *different* combination of 4 blocks. Arrange these blocks to model an amount. Record the blocks you use and the amount you modeled.

- Keep on taking 4 blocks and recording the data until you have found all possible combinations.

- Look for patterns in your data.

The Bigger Picture

Thinking and Sharing

Have children suggest how to generate a class chart to record the different amounts that can be modeled with various combinations of four Base Ten Blocks. Then set up headings for the chart and invite children to fill it in with their data.

Use prompts like these to promote class discussion:

- How did you record your findings?

- What was the greatest amount you modeled? the least amount?

- Were you able to model more 2-digit numbers or more 3-digit numbers? Explain.

- What made you think that you had found all the possible amounts?

- Did you notice any patterns? What were they?

Extending the Activity

1. Have children repeat the activity, but this time have them choose combinations of *five* blocks choosing from flats, longs, and units.

2. Challenge children to find all the combinations of four blocks, but allow them to choose from thousands cubes as well as from flats, longs, and units.

Where's the Mathematics?

Children will approach the task of choosing Base Ten Blocks in a variety of ways. Some may start by picking blocks at random. Others may develop a system for finding all the possible combinations. These children may, for example, begin with the group of blocks that models the greatest amount possible and progress to the one that models the least amount. Alternatively, children may begin by choosing four blocks of a kind and then systematically replace one of that kind with one of each of the other kinds.

The recording systems that children use are likely to reflect the ways in which they work. Some pairs may record only the numerical amounts. Others may record the number of each kind of block in a particular combination along with the amount that the combination represents. Still others may draw each combination of blocks.

Children will find that they can model more 3-digit numbers than either 1- or 2-digit numbers. They may explain this by saying that there are more combinations of four blocks for 3-digit numbers than for 1- or 2-digit numbers.

It will be exciting for children to discover that the numbers that make up the addition facts for the number 4 suggest all the possible combinations for the three kinds of blocks. That is, for the 1- and 2-digit numbers: 2 + 2 suggests 22, 3 + 1 suggests 31 and 13, and 4 + 0 suggests 4 and 40. For the 3-digit numbers: 1 + 1 + 2 suggests 112, 121, and 211; 2 + 2 + 0 suggests 220 and 202; 3 + 1 + 0 suggests 310, 301, 130, and 103; and 4 + 0 + 0 suggests 400.

Depending on how they organized their work, children may notice still other patterns. After analyzing the 15 possible number combinations shown in the chart that follows they may point out that as the number of flats decreases, the number of possible combinations increases. That is, with 4 flats only one number is possible, with 3 flats two numbers are possible, with 2 flats three numbers are possible, and so on.

Flats	Longs	Units	Amount
4	0	0	400
3	1	0	310
3	0	1	301
2	2	0	220
2	0	2	202
2	1	1	211
1	1	2	112
1	2	1	121
1	3	0	130
1	0	3	103
0	4	0	40
0	0	4	4
0	3	1	31
0	1	3	13
0	2	2	22

Children who choose to work methodically in yet a different way may start with four of one kind of block and then progress to three of one kind of block and one of another kind, then two of two kinds of blocks, and so on. Such a method is reflected in the chart below.

Flats	Longs	Units	Amount
4	0	0	400
0	4	0	40
0	0	4	4
3	1	0	310
3	0	1	301
0	3	1	31
0	1	3	13
1	0	3	103
1	3	0	130
2	2	0	220
2	0	2	202
0	2	2	22
2	1	1	211
1	1	2	112
1	2	1	121

WHAT'S IN BETWEEN?

- Place value
- Estimation
- Addition
- Subtraction

Getting Ready

What You'll Need

Base Ten Blocks, 1 set per pair

What's in Between? worksheets, 2 per pair, page 95

Small empty container

Number cubes marked 1 to 6 and 4 to 9, 1 of each per pair

Overhead Base Ten Blocks and/or What's in Between? worksheet transparency (optional)

The Activity

Overview

Children compare two numbers and then use Base Ten Blocks to help them "get from one number to the other" by finding the missing addend. In this activity, children have the opportunity to:

- ◆ develop mental math skills
- ◆ recognize that addition and subtraction are inverse operations
- ◆ find missing addends

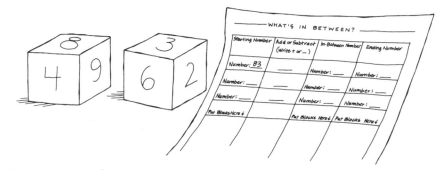

Introducing

- ◆ Display these two configurations of longs and units placing a container between them.

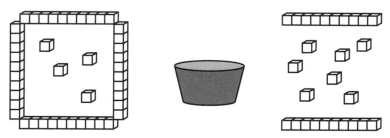

- ◆ Ask children to find the value of each group of blocks.
- ◆ Elicit that the value of the first group of blocks is 44 and that the value of the second group is 27.
- ◆ Ask children what they would have to do to change the first group so that it has the same value as the second group.
- ◆ Establish that they would have to take away, or subtract, some blocks from the first group.
- ◆ Have a volunteer take away blocks, trading as necessary, and put the extras into the container that stands between the two groups.
- ◆ Point out that the blocks in the container model "what's in between" the blocks in the first group and the blocks in the second group.

On Their Own

> **How can you use Base 10 Blocks to find how to get from one number to another?**
>
> - Work with a partner. Roll 2 different number cubes.
>
> - Use the digits you rolled to model either of the 2-digit numbers possible. This is your STARTING NUMBER. Record it on a worksheet that looks like this.
>
> | Starting Number | Add or Subtract (Write + or −.) | In-Between Number | Ending Number |
> |---|---|---|---|
> | | | | |
>
> - Take Base 10 Blocks to model your starting number. Put them on the worksheet.
>
> - Roll the number cubes again. Decide on a 2-digit number for this roll and record it.
>
> - Take blocks to model your ending number. Put them on the worksheet in the column below your ending number.
>
> - How can you get from your starting number to your ending number? Use blocks to figure it out. The blocks you add or take away model what's in between!
>
> - Write + or − in the Add or Subtract column. Then write the in-between number.
>
> - Repeat the activity 2 more times.
>
> - Now work with 2 other partners and new worksheets. (You won't need number cubes this time!) Give the other pair your first starting number as their ending number. Give them your first ending number as their starting number.
>
> - Use blocks to figure out each other's in-between numbers.
>
> - Compare your in-between number with the other pair's.

The Bigger Picture

Thinking and Sharing

Ask children to tell what they noticed when they rolled the number cubes. Call on pairs to share one of their rounds with the class, telling what they rolled and how they decided on the number, which operation to use, and what they did to find the in-between number.

Use prompts like these to promote class discussion:

- Did your starting number ever help you decide on your ending number? Explain.
- How did you go about finding the in-between numbers?
- Did you find any shortcuts for using the blocks?
- What did you find out about the in-between numbers that you and the other pair each found? What operation did each of you use?

Writing

Have children describe how they would determine the change they should get if they used three quarters to pay for something that cost 47 cents.

Where's the Mathematics?

Children approach the task of finding missing addends in different ways. You will find that some children will challenge themselves by making up the most difficult problems. Others will opt to set up the easiest problems possible, choosing the numbers they roll so that the starting and ending numbers represent simple addition examples, minimizing the need to trade blocks and trying not to involve subtraction. (If you notice this you may wish to intervene and require pairs to each set up a minimum number of subtraction problems.)

Consider the four possible problems that children could set up for the roll of a 4 and a 7 for the starting number and the roll of a 2 and a 9 for the ending number.

Starting Number	Add or Subtract (Write + or −.)	In-Between Number	Ending Number
Number: __74__	−	Number: __45__	Number: __29__
Number: __74__	+	Number: __18__	Number: __92__
Number: __47__	−	Number: __18__	Number: __29__
Number: __47__	+	Number: __45__	Number: __92__

Extending the Activity

1. Children can change the activity by rolling *three* number cubes and then work with 3-digit starting and ending numbers.

2. Instead of adding and subtracting to find missing addends, children who understand multiplication and division can do the activity by rolling two 1-to-6 number cubes and then multiplying or dividing to find the missing factors.

You may find that children use a trial-and-error approach as they manipulate blocks in trying to determine the in-between number. They may begin either with the starting number or with the ending number and then add or take away blocks, counting and recounting them, until they reach the other number. Some children will always start with the greater number and take away blocks, trading as necessary, until they reach the lesser number.

The way that children solve their problems is not as important as is their ability to understand, and be able to explain, the inverse nature of the addition and subtraction operations. The methods that children devise as they work will give you insight into their problem-solving and critical-thinking capabilities.

Round	LONGS	UNITS
1		
2		
3		
4		
5		
	TOTAL ⟶	

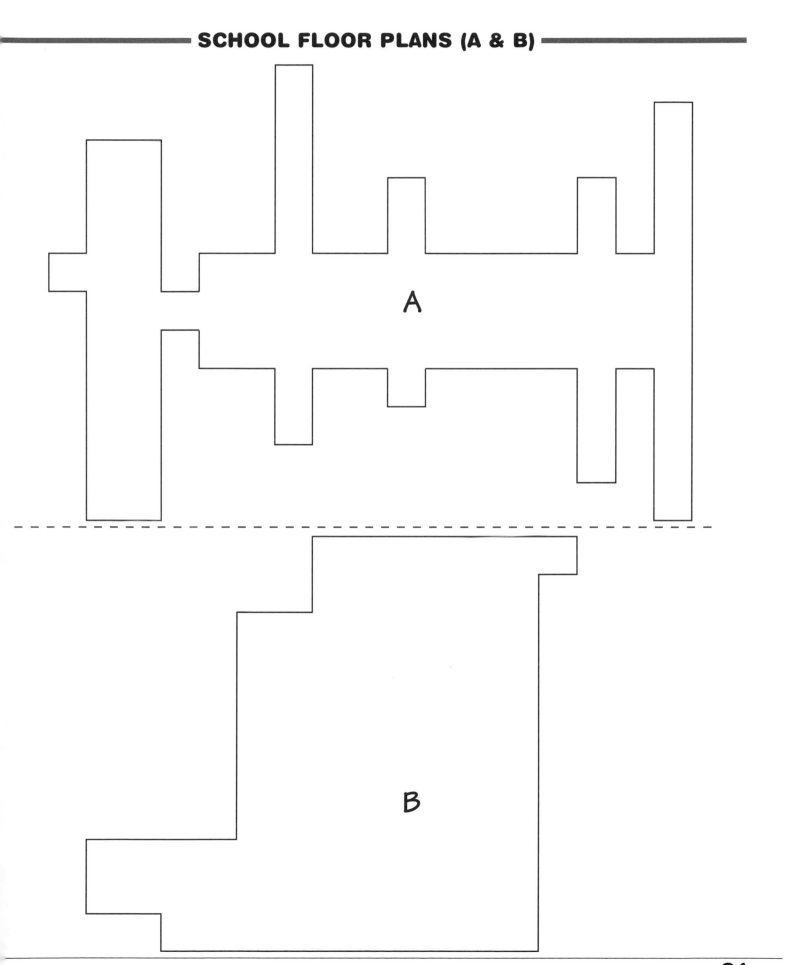

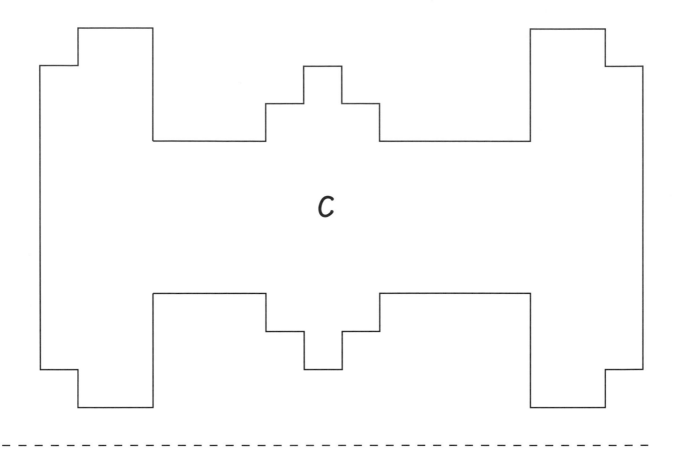

C

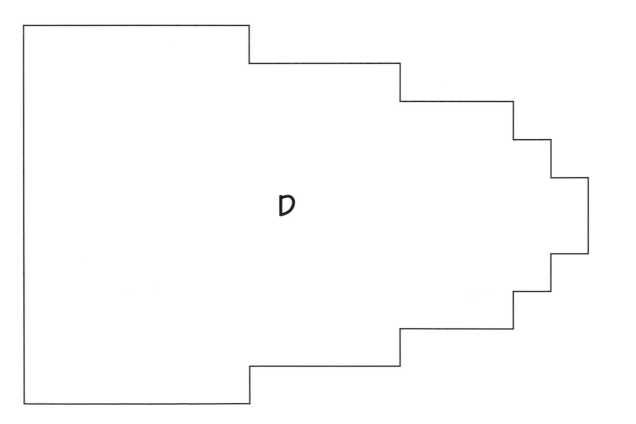

D

TEN, TEN, TEN SCORE SHEET

Round	Digits Rolled	Sum of Digits	10 Bonus Points (if 2 digits equal 10)	Score for Round
1				
2				
3				
4				
5				
6				
7				
8				
9				
10				
			TOTAL SCORE ⟶	

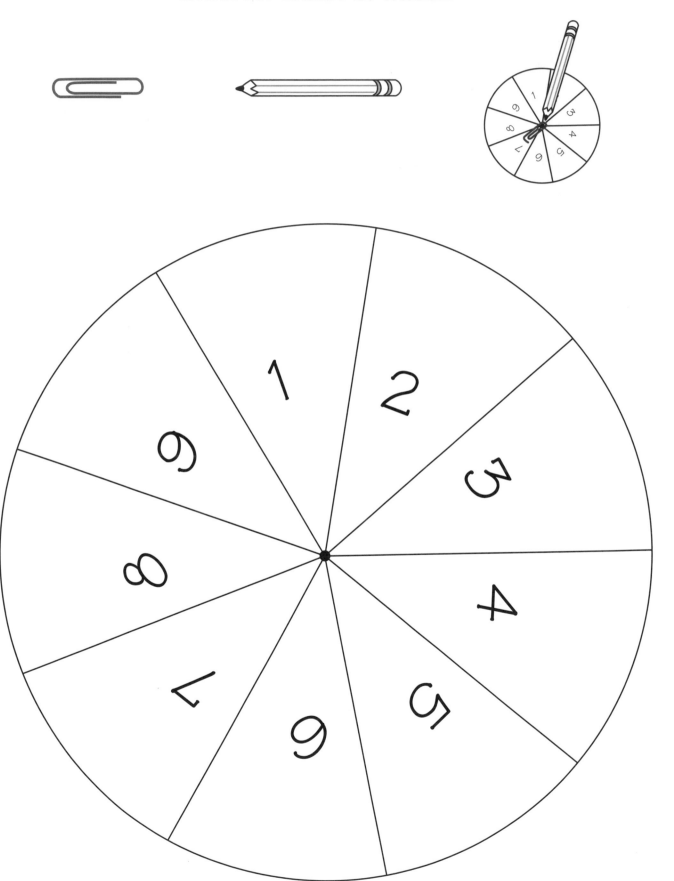

WHAT'S IN BETWEEN?

Starting Number	Add or Subtract (Write + or −.)	In-Between Number	Ending Number
Number: _____	_____	Number: _____	Number: _____
Number: _____	_____	Number: _____	Number: _____
Number: _____	_____	Number: _____	Number: _____
Put Blocks Here ↓		Put Blocks Here ↓	Put Blocks Here ↓

BASE TEN BLOCK GRID PAPER

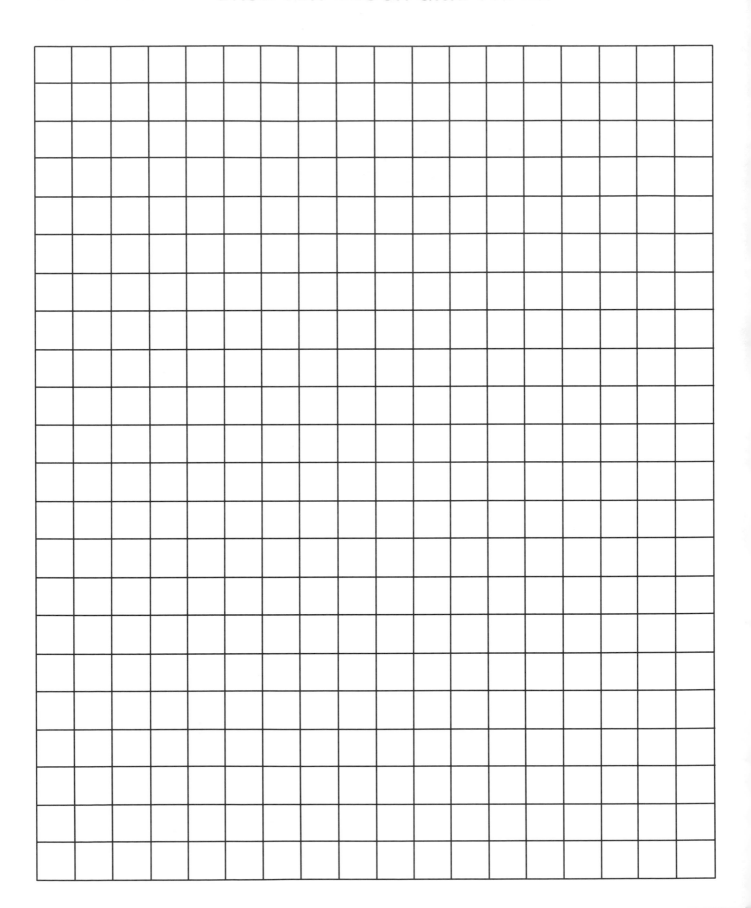

© ETA/Cuisenaire®